The Silk Road and the Cities of the Golden Horde

Zinat Press

Berkeley, California

2001

The Silk Road and the Cities of the Golden Horde

German A. Fedorov-Davydov

A contribution by
V. V. Dvornichenko

English editor
Jeannine Davis-Kimball

Russian acquisition
Aleksandr Leskov

English translator
Aleksandr Naymark

Zinat Press

1607 Walnut St.

Berkeley,CA 94709

http://www.csen.org

© 1991 by Zinat Press

Printed in Korea

on acid free paper

The Silk Road and the Cities of the Golden Horde

German A. Fedorov-Davydov

Text, B&W Plates, Catalogue, Bibliography, Glossary, Index

Color illustrations as in this volume are available at http://www.csen.org

Library of Congress Catalog Number: 2001117325

ISBN 1-885979-05-3

First edition 2001

history, archaeology
Silk Road, Golden Horde, Eurasia, nomads

This publication is sponsored in part by The American-Eurasian Research Institute, Inc. and The Center for the Study of Eurasian Nomads

Cover and book design by Jeannine Davis-Kimball

Title page illustration: Silver plaque in shape of an old man's head, Plate 19

Cover, front: Fragment of a lusterware painting depicting a person, Plate 68.

Back: upper left, gold coins of the Sultan of Dehli, Plate 42; upper right, gold ornament inlaid with colord stones, Plaste 55.

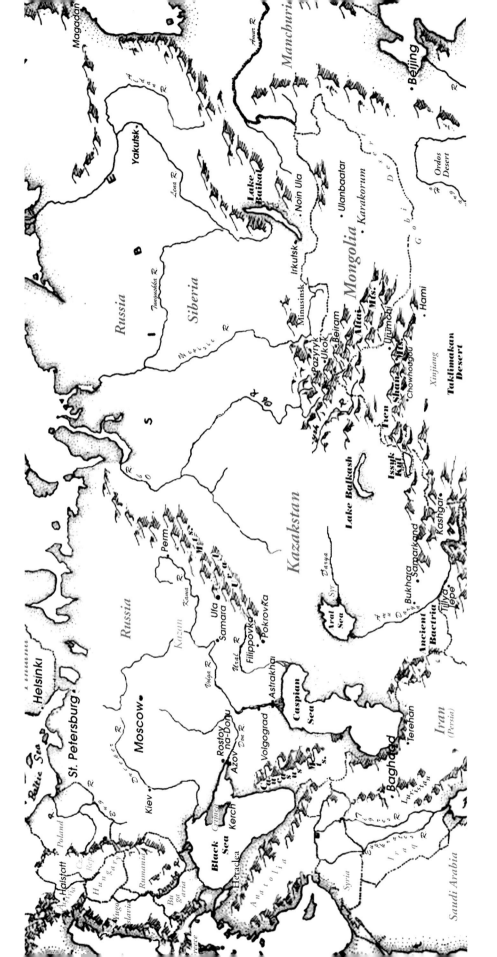

Eurasia

Biography

German Alexandrovich Fedorov-Davydov

(1931–2000)

German Fedorov-Davydov, a prominent Russian historian, archeologist, and numismatist, was born in Moscow to a family of art critics. His father Alexei Alexandrovich Fedorov-Davydov, was a professor at Moscow State University while his grandfather, Alexandr Alexandrovich Fedorov-Davydov, authored children's books and became editor of the first magazine for children in Russia. As a schoolboy, Fedorov-Davydov became interested in mathematics, but he continued his studies at the Faculty of History, Moscow State University. He loved mathematics all his life, and was one of the first to apply mathematical methodologies to archeology.

In his student years, Fedorov-Davydov's first archaeological expeditions were to the Kara Kum Desert where he worked on cities of the Medieval state of Khwarizm. Influenced by the romance of work and the beauty of ancient architectural monuments, the young archeologist was attracted forever to the East and to its antiquities. He graduated from the university in 1954 and completed postgraduate studies in 1957. Subsequently, he defended his thesis on numismatics of the Golden Horde. His doctoral dissertation, "The Nomads of Eastern Europe from the Xth to the XIVth Centuries," provided inspiration for several of his book.

During the 14th century, the Golden Horde was intricately involved in the trade between the East and the West as the Silk Route, the transcontinental trade artery between China, India, the Middle East, and the Mediterranean countries passed through many of its cities. Thus, the principal issues that preoccupied Fedorov-Davydov during the last years of his life were the connections between the Medieval civilizations in the East and in the West, and the history of the Great Silk Road.

Fedorov-Davydov was Chair of Archeology at Moscow State University for 35 years. He delivered lectures on the history and archeology of the Golden Horde, the Middle East, and the Moslem countries. His many disciples, who had attended his lectures, gone with him on expeditions, and became qualified archeologists themselves are now continuing and developing his scientific concepts.

Fedorov-Davydov authored 230 books and articles. His monographs have been translated and published in England, Belgium, Germany, Hungary, and India. "The Silk Road and the Cities of the Golden Horde, published posthumously, is his first work to be published in the United States.

Table of Contents

Biography vii

List of Figures xi

List of Plates xiii

List of Maps xviii

Introduction 3

Chapter 1. The Beginnings (with V. V. Dvornichenko) 9

Chapter 2. From the Sarmatians to the Mongols 17

Chapter 3. The Mongol Conquest and the First

    Transcontinental Journeys 26

Chapter 4. Maps 34

Chapter 5. Trade 39

Chapter 6. Money 53

Chapter 7. The Simferopol Treasure 58

Chapter 8. The Archaeology of New Sarai 60

Chapter 9. The Lower Classes 63

Chapter 10. In the Aristocratic Quarters of New Sarai 67

Chapter 11. The Excavations in Old Sarai 71

Chapter 12. Craft Shops 77

Chapter 13. City Life in War and Peace 81

Chapter 14. Religious Matters 90

Chapter 15. The Disaster of 1395 95

Chapter 16. Conclusion 99

The Plates 103

The Catalogue 143

Appendix 1. Geneology of the Mongol Khans, Khagans,

    and Qatuns 173

The Glossary 175

The Bibliographies 181

The Index 183

The List of Figures

Figure 1. Excavations of the Volga Archaeological Expedition. 1–Volgograd; 2–Astrkhan; 3–Vodiansk; 4–Chernyi Yar; 5–Tsarev; 6–Enotaevka; 7–Selitrennoe.

.Figure 2. The northern routes of the Great Silk Road. 1–Beijing; 2–Karakorum; 3–Turfan; 4–Yarkand; 5–Kashgar; 6–Samarkand; 7–Urgench; 8–Signakhi; 9–Saraichik; 10–Old Sarai (Selitrennoe); 11–New Sarai (Sarai al-Jadid; Tsarevskoe site); 12–Ukek (Uvekskoe site); 13–Bolgar; 14–Moksha (Narovchatovskoe site); 15–Azaq (Azov site); 16–Majar; 17–Hajji-Tarkhan; 18–Derbent; 19–Aq-Kermen-Monkastro (Belgorod-Dnestrov townsite); 20–Shahr al-Jadid (Staroorkhei site); 21–Kiev; 22–Constantinople; 23–Kiliya; 24–Synop; 25–Krim-Solkhat (Staryi Krim); 26–Caffa; 27–Moscow; 28–Baghdad; 29–Baku; 30–Trebizond; 31–Otrar; 32 Almalik. Double line indicates the borders of the Golden Horde in the 14th century. Trade routes are shown in dotted lines.

Figure 3. Silver plaques from horse harnesses with depictions of horsemen, Sarmatian burial at Krivaia Luka. Diameter 18 cm. (Astrakhan Historic Architectural Museum).

Figure 4. Gold plaque depicting a "Combat Scene," Siberian Collection of Peter the Great. Length 12.5 cm. (State Hermitage, Saint Petersburg.).

Figure 5. Impression of an Achaemenid cylindrical seal from the Kosika burial. Width 1.7 cm. (Astrakhan Historic Architectural Museum).

Figure 6. Sketch of a boar-hunting scene on a vessel from the Kosika burial. (Astrakhan Historic Architectural Museum).

Figure 7. Silver plaque from a horse bridle, Sarmatian burial near the village of Volodarka, southern Urals. Diameter 24.6 cm. (Ural Museum of Local Lore).

Figure 8. Depiction of a Turkic horseman on the rock of Sulek in Khakassia.

Figure 9. Turkic stone effigy (balbal). Height 120 cm. (State Hermitage, Saint Petersburg).

Figure 10. Polovtsian stone effigy of a female. Height 190 cm. (State Historic Museum, Moscow).

Figure 11. Map by Fra Mauro, 1459.

Figure 12. Decorated bone plate from a fourteenth century nomadic grave in the locality of Krivaia Luka. Height 31 cm. (Astrakhan Historic Architectural Museum).

Figure 13. Golden bracelet with "knot of happiness," Selitrennoe. Length 19 cm, width O.9 cm..

Figure 14. Gold vessel with handles in the shape of dolphins, Tsarev. Height 13 cm. (State Hermitage, Saint Petersburg).

Figure 15. Silver plates found near Volgograd. Length 8.1 cm. (Volgograd Museum of Local Lore).

Figure 16. Bronze mirror from Selitrennoe. Length 8.6 cm. (Astrakhan Historic Architectural Museum).

Figure 17. Silver goblet from the Belorechenskie barrows. Height 13 cm. (State Hermitage, Saint Petersburg).

Figure 18. Golden Horde coins, Selitrennoe. Max. dia. 2 cm. (Astrakhan Historic Architectural Museum).

Figure 19. Bronze icon with an image of St. George, found in the village of Moshaik, near Astrakhan. Height 7.4 cm. (Astrakhan Historic Architectural Museum).

Figure 20. Plan of the Tsarev site: 1–lake; 2–hillocks formed by the ruins of houses; 3–moats and ramparts; 4–fences of manors; 5–streets; 6–pits and reservoirs; 7–excavation sites.

Figure 21. Fragments of alabaster panel with the depiction of running animals, Selitrennoe. Width 8 cm. (Astrakhan Historic Architectural Museum)

Figure 22. Carved alabaster column, Selitrennoe. Height 13.6 cm. (State Historic Museum, Moscow).

Figure 23. Fragment of a carved terra-cotta tile. Width 12 cm. (Astrakhan Historic Museum)

Figure 24. Plan of a house that belonged to a wealthy family, excavated at Selitrennoe.

Figure 25. Drawing on plaster of a house that belonged to a wealthy family, excavated at Selitrennoe. Maximum dimension 11 cm. (State Historic Museum, Moscow)

Figure 26. White clay jug from Tsarev. Height 24.9 cm. (State Hermitage, Saint Petersburg)

Figure 27. Houses of commoners excavated on the Vodiansk site: 1–baked bricks; 2–adobe bricks; 3–ash; 4–stones; 5–wood.

Figure 28. Bronze mortar and pestle from the Vodiansk site. Length of pestle 13.5 cm. (Volgograd Museum of Local Lore).

Figure 29. Bronze bracelet, Selitrennoe site. Length 4.3 cm. (Astrakhan Historic Architectural Museum).

Figure 30. Left: ground plan of the mosque excavated on the Vodiansk site; right: ground plan of a madrasa in Stary Krym (Krim-Solkhat).

Figure 31. Bronze astral amulet from the Tsarev site. Height 5 cm. (Museum of the Department of Archaeology, Kazan University).

Figure 32. Double house with the remains of hurriedly buried victims of the 1395 catastrophe: 1—adobe bricks; 2–baked bricks; 3–wood; 4–ash; 5–charcoal.

The List of Plates

Plate 1.   Burials of the Bronze Age and Sarmatian Period in a barrow near Krivaia Luka.

Plate 2.   Burial of a warrior of Khazar Epoch in a barrow near Krivaia Luka, 10th century, and detail of burial.

Plate 3.   Medieval mausoleum discovered under a mound near Krivaia Luka (15th century).

Plate 4.   A large house excavated on the Selitrennoe townsite. Side room.

Plate 5.   A large house excavated at Selitrennoe. Two views [above and right].

Plate 6.   A large house excavated on the Selitrennoe townsite. Central hall.

Plate 7.   A large house excavated on the Selitrennoe townsite. Side room.

Plate 8.   Overview of a large house excavated on the Selitrennoe townsite.

Plate 9.   Aerial view of a large house excavated at Selitrennoe and bath house [center].

Plate 10.   Bath house and a large house excavated on the Selitrennoe townsite. Overhead view.

Plate 11.   Bath house excavated at Selitrennoe. Pillars supported the floor of the room that had a hypocaust heating system.

Plate 12.   Crypt on the city cemetery of 14th century, excavated on the Selitrennoe site.

Plate 13.   Buckle decorated with the depiction of sphinxes. Bronze with silver appliqué, burial near Baranovka. Catalogue No. 1.

Plate 14.   Torque. Gold, burial near Kosika.Catalogue No. 2.

Plate 15.   Torque. Gold, burial near Kosika. Detail: finials in the shape of ram's heads. Catalogue No. 2.

Plate 16.   Torque. Gold, burial near Kosika. Detail: scenes of preying animals. Catalogue No. 2.

Plate 17.   Bracelet. Gold, burial near Kosika [above]. Catalogue No. 3.

Plate 18.   Bracelet. Gold, burial near Kosika [above]. Detail: representation of carcasses of skinned sheep placed on the pelts. Catalogue No. 3

Plate 19.   Plaque depicting an old man. Silver, burial near Kosika. Catalogue No. 4).

Plate 20.   Bowl. Silver, burial near Kosika. Catalogue No. 5.

Plate 21.   Tumbler, cylindrical. Silver, burial near Kosika.. Catalogue No. 6.

Plate 22.   Vessel, called a *kubok*, with handles shaped in the form of wild boars. Silver, burial near Kosika. Catalogue No. 7.

Plate 23.   Detail of Plate 22. Handle, boar's head. Silver. Catalogue No. 7

Plate 24.   Detail of Plate 22. Handle in the form of a boar. Silver. Catalogue No. 7. Catalogue No. 7.

Plate 25.   Detail of scenes on the body of vessel in Plate 22. Catalogue No. 7.

Plate 26.   Detail of scenes on the body of vessel in Plate 22. Catalogue No. 7.

Plate 27.   Phalerae from a horse bridle. Gold, burial near Kosika. Catalogue No. 8.

Plate 28.   Detail of Plate 27. Catalogue No. 8.

Plate 29.   Belt buckle in the form of a hedgehog. Gold with colored glass and stones, burial near Kosika. Catalogue No. 9.

Plate 30.   Side view of a belt buckle in Plate 29. Burial near Kosika. Catalogue No. 9.

Plate 31.   Ornaments wih boss in center. Gold, burial near Kosika. Catalogue No.10.

Plate 32.   Finial on a large whetstone. Gold, burial near Kosika. Catalogue No. 11.

Plate 33.   Finial. Gold, burial near Kosika. Catalogue No.12.

Plates 34-35. Belt terminals. Gold, burial near Kosika. Catalogue 13.

Plate 36.   Finial in zoomorphic form. Gold, burial near Kosika.Catalogue 14.

Plate 37.   Effigy of a man. Turkish, stone-carved. Catalogue No 15.

Plate 38.   Plate. Silver-gilt, burial in the Belorechen barrows. Catalogue No. 16.

Plate 39.   Coins, part of a Golden Horde treasure. Gold, found near the village of Karatue in Tatarstan. Catalogue No.17.

Plate 40–41. Coin of the Sultans of Delhi (obverse, left; reverse, right). Gold. Catalogue No. 18.

Plate 42.   Coin of the Sultans of Delhi (obverse). Gold, Simferopol treasure. Catalogue No. 19.

Plate 43.   Coin of the Sultans of Delhi (reverse). Gold, Simferopol treasure. Catalogue No. 19.

Plate 44.   Belt ornaments. Gold, Simferopol treasure. Catalogue No. 20.

Plate 45.   Detail of belt seen in Plate 44, Simferolpol treasure. Catalogue No. 20.

Plate 46.   Belt ornaments. Silver, Simferopol treasure. Catalogue No. 21.

Plate 47.   Cast-silver belt ornaments, Simferopol treasure. Catalogue No. 21.

Plate 48.   Belt plaques. Silver, Simferopol treasure. Catalogue No. 21.

Plate 49.   Belt ornaments. Gold, inlaid with carnelian, Simferopol treasure. Catalogue No. 22.

Plate 50.   Detail of belt ornaments in Plate 49, Simferopol treasure. Catalogue No. 22.

Plate 51.   Bracelet with a Persian inscription. Gold, Simferopol treasure. Catalogue No. 23.

Plate 52.   Bracelet with zoomorphic terminals. Gold, Simferopol treasure. Catalogue 24.

Plate 53.   Chain for headdress. Inlaid with colored stones, set in gold, Simferopol treasure. Catalogue No. 25.

Plate 54.   Plaques. Gold inlaid with colored stones, Simferopol treasure. Catalogue No. No. 26.

Plate 55.   Plaque. Gold inlaid with turqouise and amethyst, Simferopol treasure.. Catalogue No. 27.

Plates 56-57. P'ai-tzü, a symbol of authority. Silver, Simferopol treasure. Obverse [top, left]; reverse [bottom, left]. Catalogue No. 28.

Plate 58-59.   Divination cup. Silver, incised, Simferopol treasure. Exterior surface [above, right]; interior surface [right].

Plate 60.   Ladle with representations of an owl and a man on the handle finial. Silver, Simferopol treasure. Catalogue No. 30.

Plate 61.   Details of the finial illustrated in Plate 60, representations of an owl and a man, Simferopol treasure [top, right]. Catalogue No. 30

Plate 62.   Case for prayer texts illustrating the "knot of happiness," top center. Gold, Simferopol treasure. Catalogue No. 31.

Plate 63.   Cases for prayer texts. Gold, Simferopol treasure. Catalogue Nos. 32, 33.

Plate 64.   Belt ornaments in Chinese style. Silver-gilt, Simferolpol treasure. Catalogue No. 34.

Plate 65.   Fragments of a vessel. Glass with enamel painting, Selitrennoe. Catalogue No. 35.

Plate 66.   Fragment of a vessel. Glass with enamel painting, Selitrennoe [right]. Catalogue No. 36.

Plate 67.   Fragments of a mosaic. Ceramic with lustre glaze [above]; tile, glazed and painted [below], Selitrennoe. Catalogue No. 37, 38.

Plate 68.   Fragment of a tile depicting a person. Painted lustreware, Selitrennoe. Catalogue No. 39.

Plate 69.   Tile sherd. Ceramic with painted lustreware, Selitrennoe. Catalogue No. 40.

Plate 70.   Tile sherds. Ceramic with painted lustreware [above], Selitrennoe. Catalogue No. 41.

Plate 71.   Tile sherds. Ceramic with lustreware, Selitrennoe. Catalogue No. 42

Plate 72.   Tile sherd. Ceramic with lustreware, Selitrennoe. Catalogue No. 43.

Plate 73.   Tile sherds with lustreware painting, Selitrennoe townsite. Catalogue No. 44.

Plate 74.   Tiles. Terracotta, carved and engraved, Selitrennoe. Catalogue Nos. 45, 46.

Plate 75.   Tile sherd. Ceramic, painted, and glazed, Selitrennoe. Catalogue No. 47.

Plate 76.   Tile Sherds. Ceramic, painted, and glazed, Selitrennoe. Catalogue No. 49.

Plate 77.   Tile border sherds. Ceramic, painted, and glazed, Selitrennoe. Catalogue No. 50.

Plate 78.   Tile with Persian inscription. Ceramic, painted, and glazed, Selitrennoe. Catalogue No. 51.

Plate 79.   Mosaic panel assembled from tiles. Ceramic, painted, and glazed, Selitrennoe townsite. Catalogue No. 52.

Plate 80.   Mosaic medallion framed by a Persian inscription. Ceramic, painted, and glazed, Selitrennoe. Catalogue No. 53.

Plate 81.   Architectural detail. Ceramic, glazed, Selitrennoe townsite. Catalogue No. 54.

Plate 82.   Fragments of a window grill. Alabaster, Selitrennoe townsite. Catalogue No. 55.

Plate 83.   Glazed bowl with the depiction of centaur, Selitrennoe townsite. Catalogue No. 56.

Plate 83.   Bowl with the depiction of a centaur. Ceramic, painted, and glazed, Selitrenne. Catalogue No. 56.

Plate 84.   Fragment of a bowl with birds. Ceramic, painted, and glazed, Selitrennoe townsite. Catalogue 57.

Plate 85.   Fragment of a bowl with the depiction of a flying bird. Ceramic, painted, and glazed. Selitrennoe [left]. Catalogue No. No. 58.

Plate 86.   Bowl. Glazed and painted, Selitrennoe[below]. Catalogue No. 59.

Plate 87.   Two sherds from bowls [bottom and right] and an intact bowl [top left]. Ceramic, painted, and glazed, Selitrennoe. Catalogue Nos. 60–62.

Plate 88.   Bowls. Ceramic, glazed, and painted, Selitrennoe. Catalogue Nos. 63, 64.

Plate 89.   Bowls. Ceramic, painted, and glazed, Selitrennoe [above]. Catalogue Nos. 65-67.

Plate 90.   Bowls. Ceramic, painted, and glazed, Selitrennoe [left]. Catalogue Nos. 68-70.

Plate 91.   Bowls. Ceramic, painted, and glazed, Selitrennoe [bottom]. Catalogue Nos. 71, 72.

Plate 92.   Bowls. Ceramic, painted, and glazed, Selitrennoe [above]. Catalogue Nos. 73, 74.

Plate 93.   Fragments of a bowl depicting a polo game. Ceramic, incised and glazed, Selitrennoe. Catalogue Nos. 75.

Plate 94.   Vase [left] and three misfired bowls [right]. Ceramic, glazed imitation celadon, Selitrennoe. Catalogue Nos. 76, 77.

Plate 95.   Sherds of a bowl with the depiction of a bird [left]. Ceramic, glazed, imitation Chinese porcelain, Selitrennoe. Catalogue No. 78.

Plate 96.   Sherds of a bowl with the depiction of a bird [top right]. Ceramic, glazed, imitation Chinese porcelain, Selitrennoe. Catalogue No. 79.

Plate 97.   Two sherds of vessels [top and bottom] depicting birds. Ceramic, glazed, imitation Chinese porcelain. Sherd of a vessel with bird's head [center]. Ceramic, incised and glazed. Selitrennoe [left]. Catalogue Nos. 80–82.

Plate 98.   Bowl. Ceramic, painted and glazed imitation Chinese porcelain, Selitrennoe [bottom]. Catalogue No. 83.

Plate 99.   Sherd of a vessel. Ceramic, painted, and glazed imitation Chinese porcelain, Selitrennoe. Catalogue No. 84.

Plate 100.   Two sherds of bowls. Ceramic, painted, and glazed imitation Chinese porcelain, Selitrennoe. Catalogue 85, 86.

Plate 101.   Bowl with an inscription around the shoulder. Ceramic, painted, glazed lusterware, Selitrennoe. Catalogue 87.

Plate 102.   Sherd of a bowl with a floral motif. Ceramic, incised and glazed, Selitrennoe. Catalogue No. 88.

Plate 103.   Two bowls [left]. Ceramic, painted and glazed. Jug [right]. Terracota, unglazed. Selitrennoe. Catalogue Nos. 89–91.

Plate 104.   Money boxes [left]. Terracotta, unglazed. Jugs [right]. Terracotta, unglazed. Selitrennoe. Catalogue Nos. 92 –97.

Plate 105.   Bowl with a child-like drawing. Ceramic, painted, and glazed, but misfired, Selitrennoe. Catalogue No. 98.

Plate 106.   Amulet with an Arabic inscription. Bronze, cast, Selitrennoe. Catalogue No. 99.

Plate 107.   Articles of daily life and commerce, (key, lock in the shape of a horse, plaque, weights, anvil, and support). Selitrennoe. Catalogue Nos. 100–107.

Plate 108.   Clothing fasteners, ornaments, and jewelry, Selitrennoe. Catalogue Nos. 108–113.

Plate 109.   Ornaments. Gold, Selitrennoe. Catalogue Nos. 114-116.

The List of Maps

Eurasia iv

Excavations of the Volga Archaeological Expedition. 4

The northern routes of the Great Silk Road 7

Map by Fra Mauro, 1459. 35

The Narrative

The Silk Road

and the

Cities of the Golden Horde

Imagine you are traveling one summer's day from Volgograd in southwestern Russia, down the river Akhtuba to the city of Tsarev, or that you are going further south through Astrakhan as far as the village of Selitrennoe, or that you have decided to cross the Volga to Chernyi Yar or Yenotaevka. Along any of these routes you might see twenty to thirty tents nestled in a small grove on the riverbank or standing in the open steppe. This would be the camp of the Volga Regional Archaeological Expedition, which has carried on fieldwork here every summer for more than 35 years (Map, Figure 1).

Every spring, amid the cares and concerns of organizing a large expedition and camp, and weary of concerns over money, food, and equipment, I often ask myself what makes me take on this burden of responsibility. A good find is a fine thing, of course, but it's a matter of luck. On a site where everything has been destroyed and nothing is clear, the most precious discovery we make might be two or three bricks

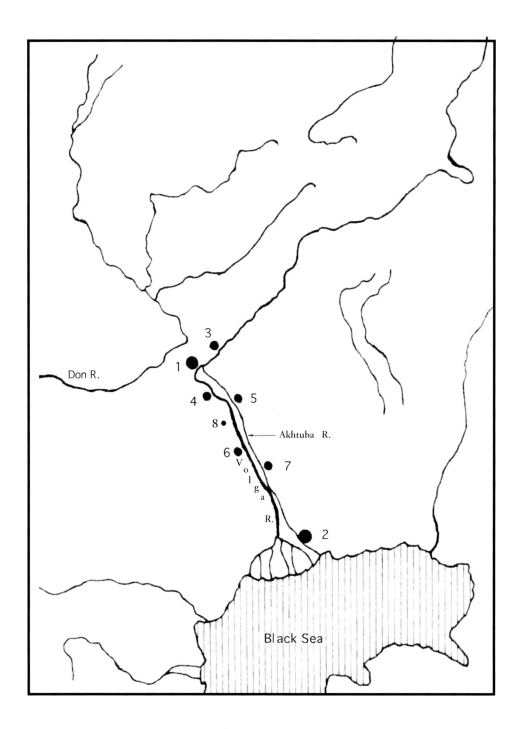

Figure 1. Excavations of the Volga Archaeological Expedition. 1–Volgograd; 2–Astrakhan; 3–Vodiansk; 4–Chernyi Yar; 5–Tsarev; 6–Enotaevka; 7–Selitrennoe; 8–Kosika.

lying in regular order, just as they were left. These are more valuable than a beautiful bowl or a golden pendant.

By September nearly everyone has left. It grows cold and rainy; the site is cheerless and depressing. Soon it will be time for me to go home, too. But these last gloomy days before leaving—or maybe even those last cold nights, when I hear the rain beating against the canvas and the wind jerks the tent pole off the ground—may be the most precious of all. During these days, all the objects we have excavated—ruined houses and shattered artifacts, broken fireplaces and filled-in pits, pottery sherds and armor from burials—all take on the kind of ghostly life I have been waiting for, in my search for long-lost times. (Plates 1-12) Sarmatian burials, the graves of medieval nomads, the city ruins of the once mighty empire of the "Golden Horde," that dominated eastern Europe for so long—all these separate things gradually merge into one great historical image: the Great Silk Road.

The term "Great Silk Road" was coined at the end of the nineteenth century by the German geographer Ferdinand von Richthofen. It proved to be a fitting title and was soon firmly established in the scholarly literature. The phenomenon of the Silk Road deeply affected the historical fate of the entire Old World. Its extensive network of trade routes, both caravan roads and water routes, eventually crisscrossed Eurasia from east to west (Map, Figure 2).

Silk was the most common merchandise of East-West trade. Light, elastic, and resilient, but beautiful, silk was highly prized in its Chinese homeland. It was easy to trade, and soon became fashionable elsewhere, in neighboring countries and far-off lands alike. Silks from China were sold in the markets of Central Asia and Iran and around the Mediterranean; eventually these countries would develop their own silk production. Other goods also traveled along the Silk Road, and more importantly so did ideas. The dialogue between East and West, at first barely a whisper, rose to a loud, clear voice. This dialogue would be of decisive importance for the future of human-kind.

Rudyard Kipling wrote: "Oh, East is east, and West is west, and never the twain shall meet." But modern scholarship has shown that East and West did at least move towards each other, despite incredible distances and the difficulty and danger of travel, regardless of cultural and ideological differences, and notwithstanding "gunship diplomacy" and colonial wars. Thousands of books have been written about the specifics of eastern cultures, philosophy, art, and religion, and about the obvious differences between East and West. Only a few dozen are devoted to the underlying similarities between historical events in different parts of the Old World—connections which helped civilizations establish contacts, and paved the way toward mutual understanding.

Cleopatra, for instance, the famed Egyptian queen, loved silk fabrics. A proper silk market also developed in Rome in the first centuries after Christ. Sycophantic envoys presented silks to foreign monarchs. Silk could bribe barbarians, pay tributes, and make dowries. It could be decorated with paintings and used to spread the word of God. In the first century of the Christian era, more than 120 ships left the Mediterranean lands for India every year, most of them bringing back silks. It was this trade that would make Alexandria in Egypt a major international trade capital, where one could find merchants and visitors from all over the known world.

Although there had been sporadic contacts between East and West further back into history, the beginnings of the Silk Road as a historical phenomenon date to the start of the common era. The southernmost branch of the Great Silk Road went from the Mediterranean Sea to the Red Sea, then on through the Persian Gulf and the Indian Ocean to the coast of India. From there ships could go on to Indonesia, Korea, and Japan. Traffic flowed in both directions: Chinese mariners exported huge amounts of merchandise, and in the 14th century promoted large-scale expansion of trade westward as far as the east African coast, where archeologists today find whole heaps of porcelain once exported to Arab trading centers.

A second route ran overland, from China through the southern lands of Central Asia and Iran, to the cities of Mesopotamia, Syria, and Palestine, and thence to the Mediterranean seaports. One branch of this road crossed the Hindukush and led to India.

Finally, a third route crossed the great steppes of Eurasia. Its network of branches started in China, and ran through Mongolia or the eastern regions of Central Asia, across the Kazakstan steppe, and on to the Volga region. From there it was a short hop to the Sea of Azov and the Black Sea, where goods were loaded on ships and sent to the countries of the Mediterranean basin, and from there distributed further throughout Europe.

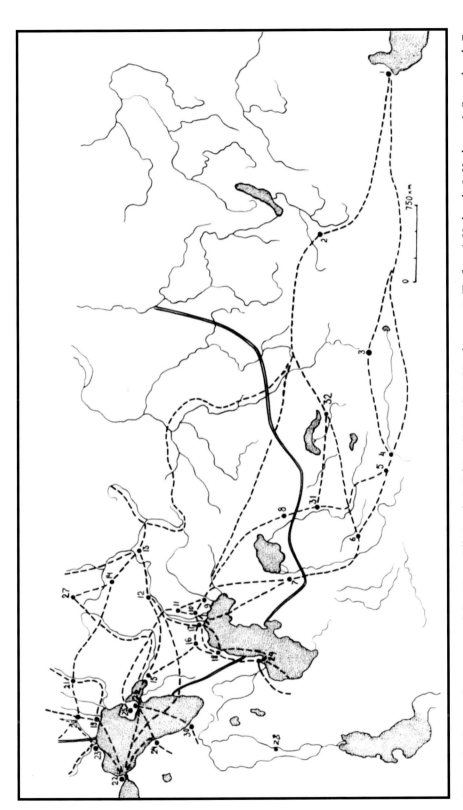

Figure 2. The northern routes of the Great Silk Road. 1–Peking (Beijing); 2–Karakorum; 3–Turfan; 4–Yarkand; 5–Kashgar; 6–Samarkand; 7–Urgench; 8–Signakhi; 9–Saraichik; 10–Old Sarai (Selitrennoe); 11–New Sarai (Sarai al-Jadid; Tsarev site); 12—Ukek (Uvek site); 13—Bolgar; 14—Moksha (Narovchatov site); 15– Azaq (Azov site); 16—Majar; 17–Hajji-Tarkhan; 18–Derbent; 19–Aq-Kermen-Monkastro (Belgorod-Dnestrov townsite); 20–Shahr al-Jadid (Staroorkhei site); 21–Kiev; 22–Constantinople; 23–Kiliya; 24–Synop; 25–Krim-Sollkhat (Stary Krim); 26–Caffa; 27–Moscow; 28–Baghdad; 29–Baku; 30–Trebizond; 31–Otrar; 32–Almalik.
Double line indicates the southern borders of the Golden Horde in the 14th century. Trade routes are shown in dotted lines.

In this book we shall look at the northern steppe route, which flourished in the 13th and 14th centuries, when the Great Steppe Belt of Eurasia was united by the giant Mongol empire. Although the empire quickly disintegrated into separate states, the impulse that had formed it continued to support contacts between East and West up to the 15th century (Figure 3).

Figure 3. Silver plaques from horse harnesses with depictions of horsemen, Sarmatian burial at Krivaia Luka. Diameter 18 cm. (Astrakhan Historic Architectural Museum)

Chapter 1
The Beginnings

In the now distant time of the last centuries before and the first centuries of the common era, nomadic tribes, related to one another in language and culture inhabited the great Eurasian Steppe Belt, which stretched from the Danube in the west to Lake Baikal and Mongolia in the east. The westernmost of these people were the Scythians; to the east of them lived the Sarmatians. Further east were the lands of the Saka, Massagetae, and other tribes, most of whom are thought to have spoken languages belonging to the Iranian family.

In our next scene, a scraper strips thin layers of soil from a kurgan (burial mound). An archaeologist follows the machine, carefully studying the fresh cut in the ground. When a patch of different color appears in the freshly exposed surface, the machine is stopped and the work continues with spades, to be followed soon after by knives and brushes. The excavation of an ancient grave begins.

Before us is a rich female burial from the fourth century B.C.E. The remains of a lamb's carcass lie by the dead woman's side—her food for the afterlife. The grave is full of jewelry: we collect more than 800 beads, along with black stone pendants in astonishingly graceful golden frames. Our most interesting discoveries are a black lacquer bowl made by a Greek craftsman, and an amphora stamped with the name of the Greek city of Heraclea. The stamp bears the name Dionysius. This burial was discovered near the dry riverbed of Krivaia Luka on the right bank of the Volga—the easternmost finds of Greek artifacts in Europe.

Nearby we found the remains of a warrior, a Sarmatian, who lived around the time of Christ. Here were buried numerous golden plaques which had once been sewn onto his clothing, along with the golden covering of a wooden scabbard, and spiral-shaped golden ornaments from a quiver. The deceased's high rank was indicated by his gold-plated belt containing scenes, apparently, from Sarmatian legends: in one of them a warrior kills a fantastic beast, behind him another man leads some animal like a horse. A rectangular open-work buckle decorated with a zigzag pattern is of the Ordos type (so called in academic literature because of the numerous finds of such plaques in the Ordos region in Mongolia). They were produced somewhere in the Mongolian steppe, which in those times was inhabited by nomadic "Huns." This is the western most find of such objects.

Another kurgan produced two beautiful silver phalerae: convex disks the size of a dinner plate, used to adorn horse bridles, and decorated with the image of an armed horseman. The mounted warriors resemble those depicted on the walls of crypts and tombstones in the Greek colony of Bosporus in the Crimea (on the site where the city of Kerch now stands), which had extremely close connections with the Scythians and the Sarmatians (Figure 3). Another find is a silvered bronze buckle depicting two fantastic animals—sphinxes, drawn in a Greek style (Plate 13, Catalogue 1).

Cultural influences from East and West crisscrossed one another in the Volga region. Following the Sarmatian nobility's rise to prosperity, steppe chieftains and warriors adorned themselves with golden jewelry, sauntered around in caftans covered with gold plates, fought with richly decorated weapons, and sheathed their swords in golden scabbards, hung on belts decorated with golden and silver buckles. By the end of the first millennium B.C.E. and the beginning of the first millennium C.E., the Sarmatians' military activity had grown. They invaded Transcaucasia, the Near East, and Central Asia. They forced the Scythians out of the Black Sea steppe and drove into Central Europe. The links between the Black Sea region and Central Asia go through the Sarmatian steppe of the Volga and the Urals.

The Kosika Burial Site

At the village of Kosika, on the west bank of the Volga about 100 kilometers above Astrakhan, the Volga Regional Archaeological Expedition discovered an extremely rich tomb that provided especially clear proof of both the extent of Sarmatian military campaigns and merchant activity, and the flow of artifacts from various centers, testifying to the meeting of different cultures and demonstrating their mutual infiltration. Here, ancient nomads had used the top of a small hillock as a burial ground. People of various tribes had already started to bring their deceased to this place far back in antiquity, and burials were conducted here until the Middle Ages, creating an extensive cemetery filled with graves from different periods. One of these burials, containing the remains of a Sarmatian chieftain or priest of the first century C.E., turned out to be amazingly rich and supremely interesting.

The deceased had been placed in a simple pit, lined with woven fabric. But the items that were put into that simple pit were remarkable. They came from all over the Sarmatians' known world, not only from countries which had been the arena of Sarmatian military campaigns, but also from those that had trade relations with the Volga region. Among them is a golden torque, or neck ornament, produced probably in the fourth century B.C.E. Its ends were decorated with stylized rams' heads, transplanted from some other piece of jewelry. The central section of the pectoral itself was decorated with scenes of lions and eagle-headed griffens with lion bodies, attacking a stag, ram, and bull, sinking their claws, beaks, and teeth into the animals' bodies. Such scenes are extremely common all over Eurasia in the nomadic art of that time (Figure 4). Pieces like this were produced for the Scythian nobility in the Greek cities of the northern Black Sea coast. This torque might have been kept in the treasury of a Scythian chieftain for many years, only to fall at last into the hands of a Sarmatian leader (Plates 14-16, Catalogue No. 2).

Another Greek-Scythian article found in this burial was a massive golden bracelet, constructed of two halves hinged together, and apparently produced in the fourth or third century B.C.E. The bracelet's open-work plates were decorated with granulation work and enamel, and depicted a row of sheepskins stretched and nailed down, with the skinned carcasses laid on top (Plates 17, 18, Catalogue No. 3). The everyday routine of a stock breeder's life is transformed here into the ornament decorating a piece of jewelry. It brings to mind the scene on the famous pectoral from the rich Scythian burial in the kurgan at Tolstaia Mogila, which shows two Scythians stretching a sheepskin, and also the myth of the Argonauts, who traveled to Colchis to retrieve the Golden Fleece.

Hellenic artwork in precious metals is abundantly represented in this Sarmatian barrow. Other products of Greek workmanship are magnificent golden plaques encrusted with the finest colored stones; another with the head of a young man, possibly a portrait of Alexander the Great, so common in Hellenistic art; and a small silver plaque shaped like an old man's face with a bald forehead, long beard, and long drooping mustache—perhaps an image of the god Pan (Plate 19, Catalogue No. 4).

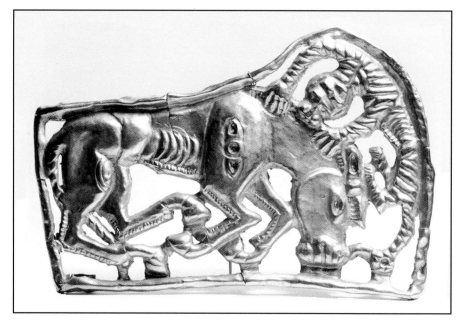

Figure 4. Gold plaque depicting a "Combat Scene." Siberian Collection of Peter the Great. Length 12.5 cm. (State Hermitage, Saint Petersburg.)

Another group consists of artifacts of Italian origin. Products of Roman craftsmanship dating from the first century C.E. were buried in this grave: the handle of a brazier shaped like a swan's head with a long, elegant neck, and a fragment of a cauldron's handle.

Alongside these articles from the Greek and Roman worlds to the west lay goods brought from the south. Beginning in the depths of antiquity, stone cylinders bearing carved inscriptions and pictures had been used in Mesopotamia and the Near East: rolled onto a clay tablet, they left impressions that were used to seal the storage of valuables, chests of documents, and treasuries. Two such cylindrical seals were found in this rich burial near Kosika. The older of the two, showing a king standing before a seated goddess, dates back to the second millennium B.C.E. Next to the image is an inscription reading "God Marduk the Great." The second, later seal was made in Iran in the fifth century: it bears the image of a king grasping the necks of two rampant lions baring their teeth, while two spearmen deal its final death blow from behind. Above the scene a representation of the benevolent Iranian god Ahura Mazda spreads its wings

(Figure 5). These seals had lain no doubt for many long years in some temple, until most had even forgotten what they were for. And then, maybe during a campaign in Central Asia or in Iran, some Sarmatian leader plundered this temple and took its treasures back to his homeland, keeping these two mysterious stone cylinders as curiosities, or good-luck pieces, until at last they were placed in his grave with his other keepsakes.

A set of engraved and gilded silver vessels found in the same grave, was probably brought from the southern campaigns. Or perhaps they were received as gifts from the kings or rulers of some peaceful southern land, in hopes of pacifying their dangerous and restless steppe neighbors. A fish appears on a silver bowl (Plate 20, Catalogue No. 5), while a small bowl has dolphins, seahorses, and fish drawn on its sides. The bowl's

Figure 5. Impression of an Achaemenid cylindrical seal from the Kosika burial. Width 1.7 cm. (Astrakhan Historic Architectural Museum).

lid is decorated with the small soldered figure of an eagle and the classic Greek meander pattern. A Greek inscription runs around the mouth of the silver cauldron, with the name of the Armenian king Artawazd, for whom apparently this entire set of vessels was originally made. The name of the silversmith who made the set is also mentioned: one Ampasalak, who had taken various vessels—some of foreign make, like the Roman bowl, and others of his own—and decorated them with his own designs.

Besides the bowls, the set contained yet another bowl with a lid, and a tumbler decorated with rosettes, fish, flying and walking birds, and hunters armed with bows

(Plate 21, Catalogue No. 6). The handles of another drinking vessel (a *kubok*) were shaped like wild boars. Their heads, including the eyes and ears, as well as their legs, tails, and hair, are finely rendered. Two bands of images decorate the body of the vessel. The upper panel contains a hunting scene: archers dressed in trousers and caftans chase huge boars with dogs (Plate 25, Catalogue No. 7). You can almost hear the barking of the hounds, excited by the hunt, attacking the prey from all sides. Below this is a battle scene: a heavily armed mounted warrior, his long hair gathered in a ribbon, uses a huge spear to stab an archer, dressed in simple trousers and a caftan (Plate 26, Catalogue No. 7). The wounded archer has fallen off his horse, but still clings to the reins with one hand, his bow in the other. The second scene shows another horseman in simple clothing, shooting an arrow. A horse, hit in the neck, falls down on its front legs. The scene is depicted with great realism and expressiveness, although the general style of the scenes is conventional: the lower parts of human bodies are shown in profile, while the torso is face-on, and the head is in profile again. Of the central figure, the heavily armed

Figure 6. Sketch of a boar-hunting scene on a vessel from the Kosika burial. (Astrakhan Historic Architectural Museum)

cavalryman, only the head is turned towards us; yet another artistic convention (Figure 6, Plate 25, Catalogue No. 7).

In this remarkable burial, items brought from the West and the South come together with those from the Far East. Some of the gold articles from the Kosika grave are similar to ones found in Siberia and Kazakstan in the 18th century, which formed the so-called Siberian Collection of Peter the Great, in the Hermitage Museum in St.

Petersburg. One such case is illustrated by a pair of large disks for decorating a bridle (Plates 27, 28, Catalogue No. 8). The disks are encrusted with colorful glass and stones, typical of Siberian art of this period. For mounting a stone at the center of each disk there is a triangular socket, which is surrounded by griffen heads with eagle's beaks. Along the edge of each disk runs a band of ornaments: a row of heads of some beast of prey, with menacing teeth in its mouth, round eyes, and large ears (Plate 28, Catalogue No. 8). Like the Scythians to the west, the Siberian nomads of this time and the Sarmatians of the Ural and Volga regions had a characteristic way of representing animals, known as the Animal Style: the objects are fairly bursting with heads, legs, horns, teeth, and beaks. The main elements of this style were to be found throughout the vast territories of the Eurasian steppe during the distant first millennium C.E.

In antiquity, belts often indicated a person's rank. The richer the belt, the higher the wearer's status. The belt found in the Kosika grave turned out to be a fairly "regal" one. Massive buckles made of gold are inlaid with colored glass and stones. They are decorated with an intricate pattern: two snakes with their tails intertwined around steppe hedgehogs. The hedgehogs' quills are made from small inlaid colored stones and glass. Larger inlays form the eyes and ears. Also decorated with stone inlay are the heads of two fantastic creatures: griffens, which appear in front of the hedgehogs' snouts. On the front of each hedgehog's body is a large red stone, while the back is formed by a single plate (Plates 29, 30, Catalogue Nos. 9).

This plate served as the base for a small vessel that was soldered to the buckles' inner side. These vessels may once have contained incense, sacred herbs, or liquids used in rituals . The Greek historian Herodotus wrote that it was customary among the Scythians to carry a vessel containing a sacred beverage on their belts. This practice apparently was also known among the Sarmatians and other Iranian tribes of the Eurasian steppe, and the hedgehog-shaped vessels affixed to the gala belt's buckles were designed to carry some such sacred beverage in front of the wearer. Depictions of hedgehogs are known in the art of Siberia and Central Asia at around the same time.

Many other golden, silver, bronze, and iron articles were also found in this last resting place of a Sarmatian chieftain, including two spears, a bow, a dagger, and a sword with golden hilt and gold-inlaid iron scabbard (Plates 31-36, Catalogue Nos. 10-14).

Another rich tomb, also that of a member of the Sarmatian aristocracy, was excavated nearby. Although it contained mainly objects of local manufacture, imported objects were also found: two disks of gilded silver—horse-bridle decorations like those we have already seen—were found wrapped in leather. They show winged griffens with eagle's heads and the bodies of feline predators, tearing apart a stag. Apparently, these plaques were produced in Central Asian workshops, possibly in the southern most province of Bactria. It is worth noting that another pair of large round bridle plaques of Bactrian workmanship was found in a Sarmatian burial in the Ural steppe region (Figure 7).

This, then, is how relations between the ancient civilizations first began. As yet, there were no secure transcontinental routes across the whole of Eurasia. But portions of these future routes were already developing, connecting Siberia with the Volga region, the Volga with Central Asia, Iran, and the Caucasus, and via the area north of the Black Sea to Greece and Rome. These connections became possible because the Eurasian steppes were already linked by thousands of ethnic and cultural ties: the tribes had similar languages, a similar way of life and thought, and closely related ideologies and material cultures.

Figure 7. Silver plaque from a horse bridle. Sarmatian burial near the village of Volodarka, Urals. Diameter 24.6 cm (Ural Museum of Local Lore)

Chapter 2
From the Sarmatians to the Mongols

The movement of goods along the Great Silk Road took various forms at different times. At first there was multi-stage trade along independent short routes; thus the Great Silk Route grew out of a system of interconnected local trade circuits. Gradually, merchants undertook longer trading journeys to carry goods over greater distances, until finally there were transcontinental journeys, for purposes not only of trade, but for diplomatic and general cultural pursuits. Even before the Great Silk Road began operating, there was already a certain cultural unity in Eurasia, elements of which can be traced as far back as the Bronze Age. And there had been sporadic exchange of goods between very distant areas of the Eurasian steppe belt over a long period.

In the Scythian-Sarmatian-Saka epoch, the cultural uniformity we have seen attests to the ethnic kinship of the peoples inhabiting the Eurasian steppe. Even then, this affinity facilitated the transportation of goods from China and Mongolia to the West and back. The Volga region became a crossroads, and goods from Central Asia, Greece, Iran, the Near East, and Transcaucasia begin appearing in burials at the beginning of the common era, as the rich burial near Kosika proves very well. Its distinctive combination of diverse objects reflects the crucial period of transition on the eve of the Hunnic invasion, which opened a new era and brought the world of antiquity to an end.

In the 4th and 5th centuries of the common era, a time known as the Great Migration Period, the movements of large masses of people became the main form of connection between the East and the West in the Steppe Belt of Eurasia. Moving westward from Central Asia, the Hsiung-nu (as they were called in East), or Huns (as the West knows them), paved the way for future travelers along the "Great Silk Road." Their route led through Jety-su (Semirechye) and Fergana in the eastern parts of modern-day Central Asia, along the river Syr Darya to the Ural and Volga region, and from there via the northern coast of the Black Sea to central and western Europe. Besides the Huns, these migrations involved many other steppe tribes and peoples as well.

From time to time the Huns waged military campaigns against Iran, or incited Central Asian rulers to attack their Iranian neighbors. They meddled in the global conflict between Iran and Byzantium, the two great powers of that age, switching their allegiance from one side to the other and extorting gifts every time. Most often, they simply plundered the natives, stealing their carts and making off with them laden with silver and gold. Then, the wagons drawn into a circle, they would dine off of silver and gold dishes and drink wine from goblets of Persian, Byzantine, Chinese, and Central Asian workmanship, while the horses, freed from bridle and harness, wandered grazing on the lush steppe grass, resting up for the next raid.

This was the nature of contact between East and West in those barbaric times. Dialogue between cultures sometimes reminds one of a wild quarrel, full of shrieking and screaming. Yet even then, there was some cultural interchange between European and Asian civilizations across the Eurasian Steppe. Conditions were ripening for closer cultural contact and for the further development of trade connections.

In 538 an envoy from the Avars—new "barbarians" previously unknown in Europe—arrived in Constantinople, escorted by a band of fierce-looking warriors, their curly hair gathered in long braids. The Emperor received him, and was obliged to suffer the following insolent pronouncement:

> The greatest and most powerful of the tribes is coming to you. The Avars are invincible, and easily crush and destroy all who stand in their path. Therefore you must make alliance with the Avars and enjoy their efficient protection. But they would only be well disposed to the Roman state [i.e., Byzantium] if you give them the most valuable gifts, yearly tribute, and very fertile land to inhabit.

Military and diplomatic relationships—sometimes friendly, but all too often ending in betrayal and treachery—eventually linked these people to Iran and Byzantium, the two mighty opposing powers that had inherited so much from the ancient world. The nomadic barbarian tribes held a middle, often shaky ground, falling in turn under the political and cultural sway of one or the other of the two superpowers. But then as now, the absence of large natural barriers on the steppe meant that the tribes could move about freely, and their campaigns strengthened the historical and cultural unity that had already existed in the Eurasian steppe in the first millennium B.C.E.

The cultural and historical unity of the Eurasian steppe and its people at this time is illustrated above all in their art. The style of the tribal aristocracy in the Migration Period is distinct from the old Scythian and Siberian Animal Style. Its best examples are seen in the numerous sumptuous objects found in hoards and the rich burials of the early and middle first millennium C.E. Along with items brought from Byzantium, Iran, Central Asia, and China, these hoards and burials contained products of nomadic craftsmen: objets d'art to suit the tastes of the new masters of the world, these "barbarian" kings and chieftains who scorned luxury, but were greedy for treasure. The glitter and shine of the gold, garnets, rubies, and enamels on these objects combined with their simple, perfect forms in a new, unfamiliar way, created both contrast and harmony. These artifacts mark the triumph of a style that emphasized simple, well defined shapes, creating an esthetic effect without the use of pictorial representation. Articles decorated in this new style began to appear in archaeological monuments of this period all over the Great Steppe Belt of Eurasia.

The Coming of the Turks

In the sixth century C.E., with the emergence of the mighty political class known as the khagans, or "great khans," the Great Silk Road became a tangible reality in the life of the steppe peoples. Their khaganate was ruled by the A-shih-na family, which derived its name from the word for "wolf," the Turks' legendary ancestor. The power of the khagans quickly spread over the steppe areas toward eastern Europe, and by 560 or 570 extended as far as the Volga.

The warlike nobility of this and later times immortalized themselves in rock art, such as that engraved on rocks in Siberia, showing racing horsemen holding their spears at the ready (Figure. 8). We also know this Turkic aristocracy from the commemorative statues, known as *balbals*, that they erected at funeral sites in honor of their ancestors

(Figure. 9; Plate 37, Catalogue No. 15; Figure 10). These people's credo is formulated on the walls of a temple in Mongolia devoted to one of the steppe leaders:

> In all we campaigned 25 times. We fought in 13 battles.
>
> From those who had states, we took away their states,
>
> We made those who had knees, bend their knees,
>
> And those who had heads, bow their heads.

In the Turkic period, the portions of the Silk Road that had emerged and developed earlier were improved, and new routes were established. The connections between West and East strengthened and took on new importance. Even when the first khaganate soon fractured into the eastern and western khaganates, these connections did not disappear, but only developed further.

The graves of the Turkic nobility contained remnants of Chinese silk—silk caftans and the like. In their Chinese campaigns the great khans took thousands of captives, to trade for ransoms of silk. In the eastern part of the steppe, Chinese coins appear in Turkic burials. Occasionally we found runes on these coins: letters carved by Turks in their ancient writing system.

Figure 8. Depiction of a Turkic horseman on the rock of Sulek in Khakassia.

Besides raids and diplomatic tours, commercial goods from both East and West moved along the Silk Road. But along its southern branches lay the stumbling block of Iran. Byzantium, keenly interested in the silk trade as well as more general mercantile interchange with the East, could count on the free movement of trade only by avoiding Iran, with its strong border guard and high customs duties. The two other options, then, were the southern route, by sea, and the northern route, across the steppes.

Some trade did pass directly from Mongolia to the Volga region via the southern Siberian and Kazakh steppes, but during this period this route was hazardous. A second variation of the northern steppe route, known from the time of the Huns, had always been more active. Starting from Dunhuang in western China and skirting the Lop-Nur basin, it led west through Khotan, Yarkand, Kashghar, and Kokand to the oasis at Shash (Tashkent).

From there it followed the banks of the Syr Darya to the Aral Sea, and then crossed the steppe to the southern Ural and Volga regions. Another branch of this route went north from Dunhuang, through the cities of Turfan and Urumchi towards Kuldja and Lake Balkhash, and then over the Kazakh steppe west to the Volga and Aral Sea region.

Travelers used both branches of the route. In the seventh century, a famous Chinese pilgrim, the Buddhist monk Hsüan-tsang, traveled the eastern section of the Syr Darya route, and troops of the Chinese Tang Dynasty used the same roads in their campaigns against the Turkic khagans. One could travel through Central Asia to Khwarizm and then cross the Ust-Urt Plateau to the Volga region, where all these routes converged. From there the road went on to western Alania, which lay along the upper reaches of the Kuban River and its tributaries, and then via the passes of the Caucasus to the ports of the Black Sea coast, where Byzantine ships waited for the goods. It was also possible to go straight west and bring merchandise directly across the steppe to coastal cities on the Sea of Azov and the northern Black Sea. The importance of these routes increased in the sixth century, when war broke out between Byzantium and Iran.

Figure. 9. Turkic stone effigy (*balbal*). Height 120 cm. (State Hermitage, Saint Petersburg)

Figure 10. Polovtsian stone effigy of a female. Height 190 cm. (State Historic Museum,

There was also movement in the opposite direction, from west to east. Envoys and trade missions left Constantinople for the mysterious and dangerous lands of central and inner Asia. In the conflict with its old enemy, Sassanid Iran, Byzantine emperors looked for allies among the Turkic rulers, who were also hostile to Iran, and had battled the Shahan Shah's armies on Iran's Central Asian frontier. A string of envoys was sent east from Byzantium to the inner lands of the Turkic khaganate. Westerners coming to the khagans' camps found Chinese silks and jewelry, as well as other products of far eastern craftsmanship, which the Turks had either received as gifts or brought home with them. When they got home, the Byzantine envoys talked of the far-off steppes, of strange customs and quaint rituals in the chieftains' camps, and of the nomads' cruelty and their courage in battle.

In 568, a Byzantine embassy was sent to Dizabul, one of the Turkic khagans. The expedition was led by one Zemarchus, whose report was recorded by a later historian:

> When Zemarchus and his companions had completed a journey of many days, they entered the land of the Sogdians. At this point they dismounted from their horses, and certain Turks, who had apparently been ordered to do this, offered them iron for sale, the purpose of which, I think, was to demonstrate that they had iron mines. For it is said that amongst them iron is not easily obtained. Thus one can assume that they made this demonstration to imply that they possessed land that contained iron.

> Certain others of their own tribe appeared, who, they said, were exorcisers of ill-omened things, and they came up to Zemarchus and his companions. They took all of the baggage that they were carrying and placed it on the ground. Then they set fire to branches of the frankincense tree, chanted some barbarous words in their Scythian tongue, making noise with bells and drums, waved above the baggage the frankincense boughs as they were crackling with the flames, and, falling into a frenzy and acting like madmen, supposed that they were driving away evil spirits. For in this way some men were thought to be averters of and guardians against evil. When they had chased away the evil beings, as they supposed, and had led Zemarchus, himself, through the fire, they thought that by this means they had purified themselves also.

> When these things had been done in this way, they travelled with those appointed to this task to the place where the khagan was, on a mountain called Ektag, or "Golden Mountain" in Greek. When Zemarchus and his companions reached the place where

Sizabul was presently staying—in a valley of the so-called Golden Mountain—having arrived there, they were summoned and immediately came into Sizabul's presence. He was in a tent, sitting upon a golden throne with two wheels, which could be drawn when necessary by one horse. After the audience with Sizabul

> . . . they turned to feasting and spent the rest of the day enjoying lavish entertainment in the same tent. It was furnished with silken hangings dyed without skill in various colours. They did not drink wine like ours, which is squeezed from the grape, for their land does not support the grape vine, and that species of plant is not native to their area. They drank their fill of another barbarous kind of sweet wine.
>
> On the morrow they met in another hut which was similarly decorated with multicolored silken hangings. In it stood statues of different shapes. Sizabul sat there on a couch made completely of gold. In the middle of the building were golden urns, water-sprinklers and also golden pitchers.
>
> On the following day they came to another dwelling in which there were gilded wooden pillars and a couch of beaten gold which was supported by four golden peacocks. In front of this dwelling were drawn up over a wide area wagons containing many silver objects, dishes and bowls, and a large number of statues of animals, also of silver and in no way inferior to those which we make, so wealthy is the ruler of Turks.

Thus the chronicler ends his description of the symbolic steppe meeting of East and West.

The blocking of Silk Road routes through Central Asia and the Near East, which started with Iran and continued under the Arab caliphates, led to an increase in trade traffic along the northern steppe routes, as the abundant archeological evidence clearly shows.

For example, silks from China, Central Asia, and Iran were found into the rich burials of Alania in the western part of the Caucasus, an area that lay along the routes from the lower Volga to the Black Sea ports, where oriental goods were loaded onto Byzantine Ships. The Alans, a powerful medieval people descended from the ancient Sarmatians, and were the forefathers of the modern-day Ossetians, and had their own way of participating in the world silk trade: they acted as guides, leading trade caravans through the mountain passes—and receiving silks in payment. Traders may also have had to buy their way through Alania, if they wanted safe passage on the road. An Alanian cemetery in the western Caucasian foothills, known as Moshchevaia Balka, preserved clear evidence of such an arrangement. Among the textiles found there, the most numerous are Sogdian silks. Sogdiana, a Central Asian country with its capital at Samarkand, imported Chinese silks to produce textiles on a large scale. Much genuine Chinese silk, however, was also found in these burial grounds.

There was a tradition of silk painting in China, particularly such art forms as silk icons. One of the burials at Moshchevaia Balka, located in the Caucasus near Nizhnii Arkhya, contained a silk painting, which after restoration, revealed images of horsemen in the mountains. A piece of paper was also found, bearing the note ". . . 100 coins . . . 10th month, 4th day . . . sold"; most probably a fragment of some accounting record. This was probably the grave of a Chinese merchant. A Buddhist manuscript was also found in the grave.

After being reworked in Byzantine workshops, part of the silk was returned eastward to the Black Sea steppe and northern Caucasus. Byzantine silks were also found here, in Moshchevaia Balka, as were small silk bags, glass lamps, and silver and boxwood reliquaries, all of them apparently of Syrian-Palestinian workmanship.

A remarkable monument of medieval Alania is Nizhnii Arkhyz, which lies in one of the mountain gorges not far from Moshchevaia Balka. Nizhnii Arkhyz was a large center of arts and crafts. Built along the route that followed this gorge towards the mountain pass and led to the Black Sea, it was one of the chief stopping points on this branch of the Silk Road, which crossed the Caucasus on its way to the Black Sea coast. Byzantium was well represented in Nizhnii Arkhyz: excavations have uncovered Byzantine coins, crosses, ivory chests, and icons. As at Moshchevaia Balka, the nearby crypts contain Byzantine and Sogdian silks. The most impressive evidence of Byzantine penetration into this area are Nizhnii Arkhyz's temples, outstanding monuments of Byzantine architecture.

Although the Great Silk Road extended primarily from east to west, north-south links to it developed around the same time. Countries united by the Arab caliphate began systematically exporting silver, in the form of money, to eastern Europe, Russia, Volga Bulgaria, and Scandinavia. The way "from Variags to Greeks" was established along the Dnieper River. Large cities like Itil and Bolgar appeared at the crossroads of east-west and north-south trade routes, and trade along the Volga and Kama rives brought articles of Iranian, Central Asian, Arabic, and Byzantine and Khazar workmanship to the far North and the Kama and trans-Uralic regions.

But now a new era began. In the 13th century, the Mongols conquered the entire Eurasian Steppe Belt, along with China, Central Asia, Iran, Mesopotamia, the Caucasus, the Crimea, Volga Bulgaria, and the better part of Russia. All these lands were subdued by Genghiz Khan and his immediate successors: his sons and grandsons. Within a few decades, this historic event would change the face of nearly the entire Old World, echoing through to its most distant corners. The history of the Silk Road entered a new age.

Chapter 3

The Mongol Conquest and the First Transcontinental Journeys

At the beginning of the 13th century, Mongol hordes charged across the Eurasian steppe like a tornado, destroying everything in their path and overwhelming the civilizations of sedentary people. Like other large nomadic migrations before it, this movement started in Central Asia, in the steppes of Mongolia. Growing economic inequality among the numerous tribes of stock breeders who inhabited these areas allowed the nobility to exploit the poorer nomads more and more, until social pressures finally reached the point when significant change became inevitable.

At this time, the family of one Temujin made its mark among the warring tribes. Temujin managed to unite all the Mongol tribes, took on the title Genghiz Khan, and directed the united peoples' energy toward the conquest of vast territories and the eventual creation of a world empire. Welding his troops together with iron discipline, Genghiz Khan led them to acquire new pastures, cattle, and slaves, and plunder flourishing oases and valleys. These wars wrought huge losses in both human life and and material destruction. In 1211, Genghiz Khan's Mongols began their successful Chinese campaign. They pillaged the ancient centers of arts and crafts, science and trade. Thousands of slaves were driven to Mongolia, where settlements of craftsmen were created to serve the Mongol army and the aristocracy. Using rich booty and enslaved craftsmen and builders, the Mongols would build new cities in the Central Asian steppe.

Another victim of the Mongols was the state of the Khorezmshahs, which had covered a vast territory stretching from the Aral Sea to the Indus Valley. The Mongol armies then invaded Iran, crossed Transcaucasia, and reached the steppe areas adjacent to the Sea of Azov. In 1223, the Russians and the Polovtsy suffered bloody defeat at the Mongol army's hands in the battle of Kalka. The Mongols, however, then turned eastward, leaving Russia in peace, but it was to be only a short respite, for they returned after a few years. By 1240 all the lands of Russia, with exception of Novgorod and Pskov, had been pillaged. In the south the Mongols subdued the nomadic Polovtsy, former masters of the east European steppe. Although by this time Genghiz Khan was already dead, these conquests were led by his grandsons, Batu and Möngke.

The capture of Russia opened the way to the rich lands of central Europe. But by now the Mongol troops, exhausted and burdened by the treasures they had acquired, could no longer marshal the violent strength that had previously let them break through any fortifications and suppress all resistance. The year 1241 saw the death of the Supreme Ruler of Mongolia, the great Khan Ogödäi, the head of all the Chingizids, or the successors of Genghiz. Batu turned his troops homeward, concerned with the possibility of sedition there.

At first, the giant empire created by the Mongols formed one unified state, stretching from China to the Adriatic Sea. In spite of the enormous destruction caused by the conquest, the existence of a single state promoted trade and helped develop a variety of ties between East and West. Later, the empire dissolved into semi-independent *uluses*—"tribes" or "small nations"—which by the end of the 13th century grew into completely sovereign states, appanages of the different branches of the Chingizid family. Iran was ruled by the successors of Khan Hulägu. Eastern Europe, Kazakstan, and Khwarizm belonged to the descendants of Jöchi, Genghiz's oldest son and the father of Batu. Their realm is what is known today as that of the Golden Horde. Central Asia formed the ulus of Chagatai, an appanage of the successors of Chagatai. The main capital of the whole empire was the city of Karakorum in Mongolia. Later, however, the grand Khan Kublai moved the center of the empire to Peking (Beijing), establishing the Mongol dynasty in China.

Rumors of the Mongol conquests and the growing Chingizid empire made a somber impression in Europe. For some, though, it raised hopes. People talked and wrote about a certain Prester John, who had supposedly created a Christian state somewhere in the East. This was an exaggerated version of some vague information about the Nestorian Christians, who had in fact lived in Central Asia for many centuries. Some people thought that the entire Mongol movement was directed by Prester John, and even believed that the Mongol invasion could be a decisive turning point in the seemingly endless wars between Crusaders and Arab Muslims. Since the Mongols had reached the Near East through Iran, the Christians expected the Arabs to be destroyed through a rear attack. In 1223, many western European knights welcomed the Mongols as the forces of Prester John. Not until two decades later, when Mongol armies appeared on the Adriatic coast and plundered Hungary and Bohemia, did the European nobility understand the scale of the threat and organize resistance against the Mongols.

The Embassy of Piano Carpini

Nevertheless, when the tide of the invasion ebbed, the legend about the mysterious Prester John was resurrected. If there were Christians in the very center of Mongolia, why wasn't it possible to use this fortunate circumstance to convert the Mongol emperor himself? So, at least, thought some in the court of the recently elected Pope Innocentius IV. And so they decided to sent an embassy to distant Mongolia. The Pope selected a Franciscan monk, Johannes de Piano Carpini, to lead this venture. A witty and educated Italian, Piano Carpini was known as a skilful diplomat, who had successfully carried out a number of difficult diplomatic missions on behalf of the Holy See.

In April 1245, the envoy left Lyons for Kiev, escorted by a small group of monks. After leaving Kiev, Piano Carpini crossed the steppe north of the Black Sea in a wagon and on horseback, finally reaching the encampment of Khan Batu near the Volga. Batu directed him further eastward, to the great khan. Apparently, the embassy passed through Urgench in Khwarizm, and then traveled to Otrar in the Syr Darya basin. From there Piano Carpini made for Central Asia, keeping to the foothills of the Altai mountains, following the northern branch of the Great Silk Road.

The grand Khan Güyük received the embassy near Karakorum, and learned the content of the papal epistle through an interpreter. When he understood that the Pope proposed to convert him to Christianity and expected him to accept the supremacy of Rome, Güyük flew into a rage. He sent back this answer to the Pope:

> By the will of the Eternal Heaven all the lands from those where the sun rises, to those where the sun sets, were granted to us. All those kings, headed by you, will without exception come to serve us and show us their obedience. From that time on we will consider you all subdued. And if you do not follow the

command of the Eternal Heaven, and resist our orders, you will become our enemies.

Although the Pope was far from pleased with this answer, he did not take his anger out on Piano, who was later appointed an Archbishop. It was then that he was able to record his impressions from the Mongolian journey, in an atmosphere of calm and quiet. Piano Carpini described the endless steppe, where such storms raged that it was practically impossible to move; nothing could be seen and the people were forced to lie on the ground. And there were such hailstorms, he said, that the water from the melted hailstones once formed a torrent in which 160 men had drowned. Each man could have as many wives as he wanted, and upon his father's death, a son could marry any of his father's widows (except, of course, his natural mother, the narrator added). His description continues:

> The dwellings of these steppe people are round in plan, and during the tribal migration they load them on carts drawn by oxen or bulls. The Tatars [as the Mongols were called] mount their idols on the carts and slaughter horses before them. The Russian Duke Michael of Chernigov was killed by the Tatars for his refusal to bow before an idol.

> Mongol men do nothing but manufacture arrows and look after the cattle; their only occupation is hunting and shooting exercises. But then they are excellent bowmen, and their children start riding horses from the age of two or three. When they are only slightly older, they are given a bow. Women ride horses as well and as long as men, without getting tired. They buy little, and produce nearly everything themselves. Women are the major manufacturers and make sheepskin jackets, dresses, and leather boots. They also pack camels and repair tents. All the women wear trousers.

Piano Carpini went on to relate how Güyük received him, and about Güyük's tent, which he called his Golden orda. This tent rested on pillars covered with gold plates, fastened with gold nails, and the top and the sides of it were covered with silk brocade. Güyük sat on the throne and everyone bent their knees before him. Among those gathered there were representatives of the most diverse people the Mongol Empire had subdued: Piano Carpini met the Russian Duke Jaroslav of Suzdal, two sons of the king of Georgia, an ambassador from the Caliph of Baghdad, and representatives of other Islamic rulers. After a long and sumptuous feast, an appointment was made for the Franciscans, and the khagan then finally received them. They were first searched and warned against touching the threshhold, for which they could killed, in accordance with the Mongols' common custom.

Piano Carpini was the first European to see an umbrella. He was shown a Chinese one decorated with pearls, one of the gifts the khagan had received. The ambassadors were asked about their presents to the khagan, and were shown how the floor of the tent was completely filled with offferings from other envoys. Carpini then went into a muddled explanation, from which it became clear that during their long steppe travel they had spent everything they had with them, and nothing was left for the khagan. How Güyük reacted to this information, the Franciscan envoy fails to mention. But he does relate that there were five carts, all full of gold and silver and silken gowns, on a hill some distance from Güyük's tent. These were divided up among the khagan and the chiefs; and the various chiefs divided their shares among their men as they saw fit. Then, after being given mead and offered cooked meat, the ambassadors were taken to another tent, all of red purple. The first thing that caught the eye was Güyük's ebony throne, wonderfully sculpted, with gold and precious stones and pearls. There were benches placed around the throne. The women of the royal house, who were all present on this day, sat in rows to the left of the throne. On the right no one sat on raised seats, but then in the middle of the tent the chiefs sat on seats of lesser height, and the other people sat behind them. Here Piano Carpini witnessed the trial of the Güyük's aunt, who stood accused of poisoning the khagan's father.

William of Rubruck

King Louis IX of France, one of the last enthusiasts of the Crusades, contemplated defeating the infidels through the help of a Mongol attack from the east. In the search for new allies, he deemed it necessary to send a new mission to the Orient, to Karakorum. To carry out this mission he chose a monk by the name of William of Rubruck, a courageous, tough, and well-educated man, who knew of Piano Carpini's experiences and other travels to the East.

Rubruck started his journey in 1253. He arrived in the Crimea by ship, and from there departed to the East. Like Piano Carpini, he too came first to the realm of Khan Batu, who sent him further on to the great khan. At this time, the position of supreme ruler was held by Möngke , who had succeeded Güyük. Rubruck did not reach Möngke's court until 1254. He tried at first to forge an alliance with the Mongols and to obtain permission to preach Catholicism, but once again the attempt to evangelize the Mongols failed. Despite the mission's failure, Rubruck's journey, like that of Piano Carpini, was to become known as one of most remarkable achievements of the time. And once again Europe gained an excellent book about the Orient, and another transcontinental trip from Europe through the steppe to Central Asia had been completed.

A talented and observant writer, Wilhelm Rubruk authored a book that even modern readers, with all our advanced knowledge, can appreciate with nearly the same interest and curiosity as the inhabitants of European cities and abbacies had when his book was first read to them seven centuries ago. Archaeologists in particular have a special interest in this work. For example, during the excavations of the ancient city of Karakorum, scholars were gratified to find that Rubruck's description of the great khan's palace matched their own findings.

On his way across the steppe Rubruck noticed effigies that steppe people had erected in memory of the dead, which were venerated as gods. He describes very precisely how these effigies held bowls in their hands, "before their navels," symbolizing their participation in religious memorial ceremonies, which were held in front of them. One can still see these sculptures in southern Russia and the Ukraine.

Marco Polo

The great Eurasian steppe, inhabited mostly by the Polovtsy, or Kipchaks, as they were called in the East, was like a great whirlwind, sucking in ambassadors, merchants, and missionaries. It dragged them, lost and confused and torn from their native lands, to the very edge of the world. The human spirit, however, was not destroyed by the blast of this wind from the steppe—the wind of history. These missionaries and failed ambassadors discovered for Europe a new world, one full of unknown countries and open spaces, of blooming islands and sandbanks full of pearls.

Many centuries ago, the masque of "Marco Polo" was a popular element of Venetian carnivals, entertaining the crowd with tall tales of exotic lands. Eventually, though, the Venetians realized that they had been ridiculing one of their most outstanding compatriots. They restored the house that had belonged to the Polo family, and nowadays proudly point it out to tourists. Marco Polo, along with Piano Carpini and Rubruck, was one of those who revealed the Orient to Europe.

Marco Polo's route followed the southern branches of the Great Silk Road. He went to China by way of Iran and Central Asia, and on his return journey he crossed the southern seas. A few years before Marco set off on his travels, his father Niccolo and uncle Maffeo went to the Orient for commercial reasons. Apparently, the two older men followed the northern variant of the Great Silk Road, arriving in the Crimea, and then setting off towards the Volga, through Khwarizm, Samarkand, and Otrar, east until they reached Mongolia. Unfortunately for us, they left no record of their travels, but their stories were retold briefly by Marco Polo and incorporated into his book.

Marco Polo's now famous travelogue is full of romantic tales of China and Japan, Mongolia, and the court of the Mongol emperors. There is much fantasy in it—as in the writings of Piano Carpini and Rubruck. But all three authors will be remembered throughout history as the discoverers of the true Orient, who brought back the first reliable accounts to Europe. And when the winds of a new age filled the sails of Columbus's ships, Marco Polo's book played its part, as the great Genoese navigator read the book and filled its margins with notes. He took it with him on his historic voyage, and perhaps searched its pages for important answers during the long nights that led up to the moment when one of his sailors spied a new land in the West.

The East, too, sent people to the West, and though we know of no transcontinental trips through the whole of Eurasia from China to Europe, we do have the memoirs of a traveler who covered half this distance: the elderly Taoist monk K'iou Ch'ang-ch'uen. Rumor of his holy life had come even to the notice of the world conqueror himself, and Genghiz Khan, feeling that his health was getting worse, ordered the monk to be brought to him. Responsible for the slaughter of thousands and preparing for new and probably even bloodier campaigns, and having interpreted philosophical discourses concerning eternal serenity and tranquility too literally, Genghiz Khan had suddenly determined to find the "elixir of eternal life." Ch'ang-ch'uen, whose name means "Eternal Spring," responded to the emperor's summons and set off for the West, intent on persuading the Great Conqueror to establish peace. Traveling through Mongolia and northwestern Central Asia, he finally reached Samarkand, following one of the northern branches of the Great Silk Road.

Ch'ang-ch'uen describes good roads, and wooden and stone bridges over the rivers. He found Samarkand ruined by the Mongol destruction, with only a quarter of the population spared, and reported that the governor spoke Chinese. This was in the year 1222. Despite all the losses, the bazaars were functioning and there were outdoor festivities on public holidays, as well as nighttime feasts during the fast month of Ramadan. At the same time, hungry peasants were wandering around the city, and gangs of robbers were gathering.

Finally, the meeting between the Chinese monk and the Mongol conqueror of the world took place. Answering Genghiz Khan's question concerning eternal life, Ch'ang-ch'uen said: "I have means of protecting life, but no elixir that will prolong it." If Genghiz Khan was disappointed, he did not show it. He summoned the monk several times, and ordered what he said to be recorded. When Genghiz fell from his horse during a hunt, injuring himself and narrowly escaping the fangs of a furious wild boar, Ch'ang-ch'uen tried to use the opportunity to persuade the ruler to refrain from hunting and war-mongering. For several month Genghiz Khan did abstain from hunting, either because of the strength of the Taoist monk's words or his own advancing age. The old hermit then left his all-mighty interlocutor and went home. On the way home, he used the post road that led to the eastern slope of the Mongol Altai. By 1224 Ch'ang-ch'uen was back in China. He had covered in all several tens of thousands of li—about 12,000 kilometers—through difficult places unknown to the Chinese. Genghiz Khan sent a message after Ch'ang-ch'uen and its seems that the haughty lord of half the inhabited world had come to love this old Chinese man:

> Holy adept, between the spring and summer you have performed no easy journey. I wish to know whether you were properly supplied with provisions and remounts. At Hsüan-ti and the other places where you have lately stayed, did the officials make satisfactory provision for your board and lodging? Have your appeals to the common people resulted in their coming over to you? I am always thinking of you and I hope you do not forget me.

There were many Chinese in Genghiz Khan's administration. He made the astrologer, Yeh-lü Ch'u-ts'ai, his minister. The Chinese travelled along the Mongol post roads, conducting censuses and collecting taxes.

Representatives of the subjugated peoples also promoted east-west contacts. Muslim merchants were a major source of information on the state of affairs in Central Asia and Iran. There were many descendants of the aristocratic Kipchak families at the Chinese court of the Mongol khans. Among them were Polovtsy, who knew the western steppe well and were aware of what was happening in Russia, the Caucasus, the Crimea, and Byzantium.

Chapter 4

Maps

This, then, is how East and West came closer to one another. Western travelers gave accounts of their experiences in the lands of the Far East. In the East, likewise, knowledge of the West and the Middle East—which was the West for China—increased gradually, and was reflected in Chinese maps of the world, for example one of 1330, which began to give notice of how vast and diverse the world really was. In both East and West the work of making these maps went on apace, so that the 14th century could be called the age of "the rise of cartography."

In the West, the most enterprising people of this time were the Italians, whose maps showed the shores of oceans and the locations of port cities, and also outlines of the Eurasian interior. Several such maps and even atlases of the 14th and 15th centuries are known to us: for example that of Pizzigani in 1367, the Catalon Atlas of 1375, and Fra Mauro's of 1459. Many of their details, especially concerning the remoter regions, are based on guesswork, or old information that was already outdated when the maps were drawn. But for all that, they represented a remarkable glimpse of terra incognita. Not only the northern Black Sea steppe, the Volga region, and the area of modern Kazakstan are there, but also the lands of central and even eastern Asia. The Catalon map, for instance, marks the lands of Gog and Magog, India and the Indian Islands, Khanbaligh (the capital of the Mongol Emperors in China), and an Armenian monastery in the Far East where relics of St. Matthew were preserved. It showed islands "having many fine gyrfalcons which are caught and supplied exclusively to the court of the grand khan," and the fabled country of women, and a city "destroyed by snakes." Reality and fantasy are mixed in these maps, as tales about people with dogs' heads and humans with three eyes are combined with accurate information about geography, customs, and the history of Asian countries taken from European travelers' accounts of the 13th and 14th centuries.

But there is genuine cartographic data, information about the cities on the Volga built by the khans of the Golden Horde. Let us look at Fra Mauro's map (Figure 11). It is easy to recognize the Caspian Sea, which is drawn quite accurately. A whole network of rivers flows into it. The Volga was called the "Edel" and shown with its complex delta. A small fortress appears on the lower course of the Volga: this was the Golden Horde site of Hajji-tarkhan. In the 14th and early 15th centuries this city was on the right bank, and Astrakhan was built later on the left.

Further up the Volga delta there are two places named Sarai (Saray on map). The first Sarai is near the Caspian, and is the first capital, which Rubruck saw and which was built in the time of Batu. Today, what is left of this city is called Selitrennoe Gorodishche (literally "Saltpeter town-site"), a huge archaeological site lying in the neighborhood of Astrakhan. Above this the map places "Sarai Grande" or

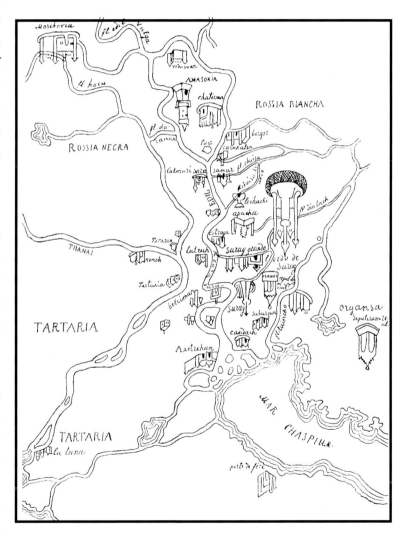

Figure 11. Map by Fra Mauro, 1459

"Great Sarai," and now known as New Sarai. This was the second capital of the Golden Horde; it was built under Khan Özbeg in the 1330s, flourished under the next khan, Janibeg, and went into decline after Tamerlane's invasion in 1395. This city, too, left a large town-site, known as Tsarev, in the Volgograd oblast.

Nearby, the map shows the Golden Horde city of Beljamen, which matches the archaeological site of Vodiansk, near the modern city of Dubovka above Volgograd. Further up the left bank, it depicts a large palace with three towers, which a caption calls the "Orda of Sarai." An orda, apparently, was a temporary camp that served as a khan's headquarters. At the mouth of the Don (the Greek Tanais), is Tana—the Italian name for the Golden Horde city of Azaq, where Venetian and Genoese merchants had their own trading colonies. Some maps mark the major Golden Horde cities with flags bearing the family crest of the ruling dynasty of the Jöchids, the descendants of Genghiz Khan's son Jöchi.

Not far from the "Orda of Sarai," the map shows the Graves of the Emperors, whose actual location is unknown. The Aral Sea is depicted very small, and beyond it the map marks Urgench—the major city of Khwarizm in the time of the Golden Horde supremacy. The map shows Bolgar, the capital of Volga Bulgaria, near the confluence of the Volga and Kama, as well as Moscovia, and also the mythical Amazonia.

The Italian maps, however, do not show all the Golden Horde cities, and even omit some of the largest. For example, there was the city of Ukek on the Volga, whose ruins are preserved close to the present-day Saratov, near the village of Uvek. Another large Golden Horde city, called Majar, was situated in the northern Caucasus. The modern town of Stary Krim rests on the remains of Krim-Solhat, which was the center of the Crimea during the Golden Horde period. There was a Shahr al-Jadid, the "New City," in Moldova, and the stronghold of Mokhsha was built in Mordvinia. The fortress of Saraichik stood on the road from Sarai to Khwarizm. A branch of the Jöchids ruled the cities of Signakhi, Sawran, and Jand, along the Syr Darya (Map, Figure 2).

The Cities of the Golden Horde

The cities of the Golden Horde were a unique historical phenomenon. Among the Mongol empire's ruling class, there were some who understood the need to shift away from their traditional raiding and pillaging of sedentary city dwellers, toward the systematic, peaceful exploitation of an urban population. As a result, the nomadic aristocracy of the uluses gradually switched to a new policy of promoting crafts and trade. And soon, like bubbles in yeast, cities began to spring up among the Golden Horde. At first, these cities were conquerors' strongholds and administrative centers. These were the "sedentarized" headquarters of the khans, surrounded by the palaces of the aristocracy. They later expanded to include housing for slaves, other dependents, craftsmen, and freedmen.

The strong centralized power of the Khans supplied these new cities with manpower by bringing in craftsmen from conquered countries, and also provided relative safety on the trade routes, creating an environment in which cities could survive without fortifications. The khans even forbade cities to have walls. Only in the second half of the 14th century, when the country entered a period of internecine wars, did some of the Golden Horde cities erect defenses, albeit rather weak and poor ones. As soon as the strong central powers began to decline, the cities withered. The nobility, divided into factions, entered into bloody wars. In the cities, the dignitaries of the various khans and their challengers eliminated one another in their thirst for power.

The orda, the mobile headquarters and official royal residence, remained the favored, if not obligatory, base of operations for the khans. Throughout the year this giant "city on wheels" would move around the steppe with its assemblage of mosques, craft shops, and markets, presumably coming closer to the "sedentary" city capitals in winter. The steppe saw a magnificent flowering of the typical oriental urban culture, a culture quite alien to the nomads—one of glazed bowls and mosaiced mosques, of Arab astrology, Persian poetry, and Islamic religious scholarship, of interpreters of the Holy Qur'an, mathematicians and algebraists, of highly refined ornament and calligraphy. But this culture was short-lived; it failed to take root in the traditional nomadism of the lower Volga region.

The Mongols themselves, and the entire population of the Golden Horde, came to be known as the Tatars, after one of the Central Asian tribes. Meanwhile, the conquering Mongols began to open themselves up to their surroundings. The cities of the Golden Horde were inhabited by Polovtsy, Bolgars, Russians, natives of Central Asia, the Caucasus, and the Crimea and it was their hands that built the urban culture of the Golden Horde.

As the pace of these developments began to grow, the rise of the Mongol empire promoted further contacts, especially those of international trade, between East and West. The connections were now based on the strong Chingizid government, rather than on the nomads' ethnic ties and migrations, or on loose political alliances as with the Turkic khaganates. As in earlier times, the Volga region retained its special position as a transition zone between the western and eastern parts of the Great Eurasian Steppe Belt, as the rich Sarmatian burials near Astrakhan have already shown us. We will see now that the same holds true for the city culture of the Golden Horde. Moreover, the lower reaches of the Volga were key areas for trade along this river, for it was the crossroads of the east-west Silk Road and the north-south Volga route. Khan Batu, the founder of the Golden Horde, recognized this fact when he chose the Volga Delta as the site of his capital.

The cities of the Golden Horde became the most important centers on the Great Silk Road. And like Alexandria many centuries before, they were cosmopolitan cities, where people from the most diverse and distant countries came together. This factor influenced the culture and daily life of these cities, and is reflected in the artifacts archaeologists have unearthed in their ruins: porcelain imported from the Far East, a coin minted by a crusader ruler of Beirut, an Italian pharmaceutical vessel and a glass lamp from Egypt, glazed pottery following the fine traditions of Central Asian and Iranian craftsmanship, and Russian pots, Arabic amulets, and Christian crosses and portable icons.

Chapter 5
Trade

The khans and the aristocracy encouraged trade. After all, they received large profits from it, as investment in trade and crafts was a practical way to use the treasures they obtained by plunder. Large merchants' associations were in a position to organize large-scale international trade, and financiers were available to subsidize it. The khans also provided merchants with charters offering them protection, and the merchants in turn often supplied the khans with money. The state provided a postal service and ensured safety on the roads. The imperial postal service existed from the 13th century on, with posting stations (called *iams*), a guard service, relays of horses, and food supplies. Balducci Pegalotti, a 14th century financier from Florence, wrote of the route from the mouth of the Don to China that:

> . . . according to the words of merchants who have accomplished this journey, the road is quite safe both by day and by night; only if a merchant should die on the way there or back, all his property is handed to the lord of the country in which he died, and it will be taken over by his officials; but if it should prove that there should be with him a brother or close friend who can say that he is a brother of the deceased, then the property of the deceased will be delivered to him, and in this way it will be saved.

As we can see, everything is organized in quite a civilized manner.

During this time, trade galleys were plying all over the Black Sea and the Sea of Azov. There were a number of Italian colonies, mostly Genoese, in the Crimea as early as the 13th century. The Arab, Ibn al-Athir, writing in the same century, relates of the Crimean city of Sudak: "Ships dock there with clothing; the latter is sold, and with the proceeds they buy girls and slaves, black fox, beaver, gray-squirrel skins, and other products." William of Rubruck described the goods imported and exported through the Crimean ports in the 1250s, especially via Sudak:

> Thither come all the merchants arriving from Turkey who wish to go to the northern countries, and likewise those coming from Russia and the northern countries who wish to pass into Turkey. The latter carry marten and gray-squirrel skins, and other costly furs; the former carry cotton or bombax, silk stuffs, and sweet-smelling spices.

One important Crimean trade center and warehousing site was Caffa where the modern city of Feodosiya is located. Trade between Caffa and the Golden Horde city of Krim, where goods were purchased on arrival from the Orient, went through the hands of the wealthy merchant families of Caffa, who then traded with Genoa. Wine and fruit were brought from Caffa to Krim, and western European textiles, Italian glass, armor, majolica, silver, and paper went to the cities of the Volga region and Russia through Caffa. Rice and spices were taken from Caffa to the Golden Horde. Oriental goods like pearls, incense, and spices that came to Caffa were transported either through the trade routes of the Golden Horde, or through Asia Minor (Map, Figure 2).

The cities of Aq-Kermen—known also by the Italian name Moncastro and the Russian Belgorod Dnestrovskiy—and Kiliya, on the lower Dniester and the Dnieper, had stable connections with Constantinople, Sinope, and Trebizond. Like the Crimean cities, Aq-Kermen and Kiliya exported wood, wax, furs, wheat, millet, barley, sugar, salt, cheese, fish, caviar, lard, and smoked food. Fragments of glazed pottery with golden-hued lustre and blue paint have been found in Belgorod Dnestrovskiy, and similar Spanish vessels have also turned up in other Golden Horde cities of the Crimea and Volga region. At Belgorod Dnestrovskiy, archaeologists have discovered a beautiful Italian glazed bowl with a human face in profile, fully in the spirit of the early Italian Renaissance. The archaeological material from Belgorod Dnestrovskiy also includes items of Genoese origin, Byzantine and Bulgarian pottery, and glass imported from the Near East.

The so-called Moldovan trade route, which led north to Poland via Lvov and further on to the Baltic Sea, started in Caffa, Kiliya, and Aq-Kermen-Monkastro, attracting Genoese, Tatar, Alan, Jewish, Armenian, and other merchants to these cities. This

Moldovan route acquired particular importance in the 14th and 15th centuries, when the unstable situation in the steppe led to the decline of trade along the road through Kiev. Slaves, grain, cattle, and salt were exported through Moncastro, and ceramics from Poland—which turn up in the Golden Horde strata of Moldovan archaeological sites—were also brought via this route. Oriental spices and silks passed through Moldova from south to north. Among other goods moving along this route were wax, silver, luxury objects, and cattle. At the beginning of the 15th century, the Golden Horde exported oxen to Poland, Wallachia, Transylvania, Germany, and Italy. Felt, various metal articles such as knives and armor, and other merchandise from the cities of Central Europe were carried south from Lvov.

Contacts between East and West were especially close in Caffa, Sudak, and Moncastro, as merchants from Genoa, Venice, and other Italian towns came in contact with Asian traders and were introduced to all sorts of products from the limitless expanse of Asia—at a time when the Italian Renaissance was just beginning. People already influenced by new a view of the world, and a new understanding of their place in this society, now looked into the "slanted, greedy" eyes of the Mongols.

This sense was especially evident in the Golden Horde city of Azak, at the mouth of the Don, where the Italian colony of Tana was situated. In the mid-14th century, it became a bone of contention between Genoa and Venice, leading to war between those mercantile empires. According to the peace treaty of 1355, both the Genoese and Venetians agreed not to dock in Tana for three years, after which this city was to become a free trade zone for both Italian republics. There was also a Greek quarter in Tana. Balducci Pegolotti names goods that were coming to Tana by different routes in the 14th century: iron, tin, copper, ginger, pepper, saffron, gold, pearls, amber, silk, brocade, cotton, linen, flax, leather, beeswax, hemp, wine, vegetables, wheat, rye, sturgeon and caviar, suet, cheese, oils, honey, furs, and pelts. Venice sent cloth, canvas, and linen. The 14th century writers also reported that Italian merchants were exporting to Tana linen and cotton textiles from Syria, raw cotton and cloth from Languedoc, Toulouse, and other places, silver ingots, copper, tin, iron, and wine from Greece and Naples, and carpets, fustian, dyed goatskins, walnuts, sugar, mercury, cinnabar, amber, frankincense, madder, luxury items, and silver and gold tableware. From Tana they brought back to Venice, among other things, silk, pelts, beeswax, furs, spices, sandalwood, nutmeg and mace, and medicines.

Especially bustling were the trade connections between Tana and Trebizond, where the Venetians were also in charge. The chancellery of the Venetian senate carefully registered the number and cargoes of all ships departing from St. Mark's Republic for Trebizond and Tana, as well as the volume of goods imported from these colonies. The fine glazed ware from Iran and Asia Minor that archaeologists find in the Crimea was brought through Trebizond and other southern Black Sea coast cities in the 13th and 14th centuries.

The export of grain from northern Black Sea coast ports to the west and south depended on the political climate and stability of the Golden Horde. The khans encouraged Italian trading enterprises on the Black Sea, while at the same time controlling and exploiting them by imposing high customs duties. In 1333, Khan Özbeg signed a treaty with the Venetians regarding trade in Tana; the city's fortifications were erected at this time. In 1343, Khan Janibeg banished the Venetians from Tana, although trade relations with them were restored in 1347. The 14th and 15th centuries were times of conflict when the Golden Horde forced Caffa to buy all its grain from Trebizond, Sinope, and other southern Black Sea cities. As a rule, grain prices in Caffa and Trebizond were lower than those in Italy.

Egyptian tradesmen and geographers, too, were familiar with the routes to the Golden Horde through the Black Sea and the Sea of Azov. Al-Kalkashandi, an Arab geographer of the early 15th century, describes numerous harbors on the northern and eastern Black Sea coast and on the Sea of Azov: Chersonesus, Sudak, Caffa, Kerch, Azaq, Abkhas, Sukhumi, and Taman.

The cities of Krim and Azaq served as gateways for the Golden Horde capitals' active trade with the circumpontic area and Mediterranean lands like Egypt and Italy. Among the valuables exported from the interior regions of the Golden Horde and the cities of the steppe zone to the coastal cities of the Black Sea were slaves. The Arab geographer al-Umari wrote in the 14th century: "From those Kipchaks comes the major part of Egypt's troops, for the Sultan and the Emirs of Egypt have been drawing upon them since the times when al-Malik as-Salikh Najm ad-Din Ayyub started eagerly buying Kipchak slaves." Among the Golden Horde, impoverished parents sold their children into slavery, to be brought to the Black Sea cities for sale by merchants. These ports were the endpoints of the Golden Horde slave trade, but human merchandise was also bought and sold in Sarai itself. Besides Turks, people of Finno-Ugaric stock and Russians were also traded on these markets.

Goods arriving down the Volga from the north and east also ended up in the Black Sea ports. Leather and furs, silk and other expensive textiles, dyes and gems, as well as various spices and medicines were transported to the West. Some types of silk were called "Urganjian" or "Khwarizmian" because they were delivered to Sarai through Khwarizm. Fish and caviar were brought to Sarai, and rice, precious stones and pearls, brocade, saffron, and medicines were also exported through the city from Central Asia.

The direct route from Azaq and Krim to Sarai cut aross the steppe. To reach New Sarai, it was necessary to go to the crossing point where the Volga and Don flowed close to one another. An alternate route led along the Caucasus to Hajji-tarkhan, and then up the Volga to Sarai. One branch of this southern route split off to the north Caucasian steppe and led to Transcaucasia and Iran via Derbent (Map, Figure 2).

Some information has survived regarding trade and diplomatic missions from the cities of the Black Sea area to Sarai. For example, in 1338, a papal envoy to China, Giovanni Marignoli, began his trip from Avignon, going on to Caffa, and proceeding from there to Tana and New Sarai. Then he traveled to Urgench, most likely via Saraichik. In 1374, the Genoese merchant Lucino Arrigo left Tana and reached Sarai after crossing the Don and the Volga. Thereafter he traveled down the Volga to the Caspian Sea. In 1391 and 1392, a Venetian merchant, Pietro Stronello, traveled from Tana to Hajji-tarkhan. These successors of Carpini, Rubruck, and the Polo family now enjoyed better traveling conditions than their predecessors, who had had to cross an open steppe devoid of cities or other settlements save the camps of nomads or the headquarters of khans. During the course of the century, the cities that had sprung up in the steppe, though scattered, were important, for there the traveler could rest comfortably and even look forward to an occasional meeting with a fellow countryman. In those days, the road from Tana to Hajji-tarkhan took twenty-five days by oxen, or ten to twelve days on horseback. The trip from Krim to the Volga took twenty days.

The Black Sea trade with the Golden Horde was especially important for Europe since the older oriental trade routes, the southern variants of the Great Silk Road through the Near East, were lost after Muslims defeated the Crusaders in the 12th and early 13th centuries. In the 13th and 14th centuries, these southern routes never regained their previous significance, because of conflicts between the Golden Horde and Iran and Egypt and Iran. The khans of the Golden Horde were, however, quick to establish diplomatic and religious ties with the rulers of Egypt. This also helped to encourage trade on the northern routes leading through the Black Sea and Eurasian steppe.

The Golden Horde cities of the lower Volga and the north Caucasian steppe show evidence of trade contacts with the West. There are amphorae—double-handled vessels for carrying liquids—from Tana, Trebizond, and Krim, some of them bearing impressions of stamps in Greek script. A fragment of an amphora found at Selitrennoe is stamped with a Latin inscription and a picture of a lion; this one could have come from Venice. A lead seal with a cross was also found, obviously of western provenance, and Byzantine and Venetian glass also occur there. In one of the Volga cities, a bronze support was discovered (Plate 107, Catalogue No. 105) that has an exact counterpart in the material excavated from the Byzantine city of Corinth in Greece. A brass apothecary's mortar of western European manufacture was discovered in Majar.

There are also articles from Egypt, such as an inscribed marble candlestick found on the site of Tsarev. Fragments of magnificent glassware have been discovered, oil lamps with enamel painting that are typical of those produced in the workshops of Cairo. Fragments of other types of fine glass vessels with enamel decoration occur among finds in the archaeological strata of the cities (Plate 65, Catalogue No. 35). A large piece of a glass dish found at Selitrennoe had enamel painting of the Near Eastern type, depicting four cranes surrounded by leaves and fruit (Plate 66, Catalogue No. 36). Intact vessels of this kind were retrieved from the burial grounds near Stanitsa Belorechenskaia on the river Kuban. Other evidence for trade contacts with the Mediterranean world was also discovered there: two finely decorated deluxe silver dishes, one from Raguza (Dubrovnik) on the Adriatic Sea, the other of Italian workmanship (Plate 38, Catalogue No. 16).

Pottery bowls produced in the Golden Horde cities of the Volga also occur in Byzantium. For example, such bowls were placed as decoration in the walls of a church in Thessaloniki in northern Greece.

Products from Egypt and other countries of the Mediterranean basin could also come to the Golden Horde as gifts. Treaties between the khans and Egyptian rulers contained clauses granting special privileges to the merchants of both nations, and we know that the Egyptian sultans sent presents to the khans of the Golden Horde, allies in their constant confrontations with Iran. Arab writers recorded impressive lists of these presents, which included all the luxury items of the Orient, articles of Italian workmanship, exotic animals, slaves and slave-girls, each one as beautiful as the next, gems, and religious objects. One tires of reading these seemingly endless lists of gyrfalcons, precious armor, and white hare skins.

The flow of western products from the countries of the Mediterranean basin also provoked imitations in the Golden Horde cities, and affected styles in local craftsmanship. Some of the jewelry found in the Golden Horde territory shows traces of European influence, mainly Italian.

The Road to Khwarizm

The eastward road from Sarai went to Saraichik, and from there across the Ust-Urt Plateau to Khwarizm and cities in other Central Asian countries. There is pottery brought from Khwarizm in the Golden Horde cities, and jars from the Volga region among the finds in Urgench. Khwarizmian vessels carved from soft talcochlorite stone are found in the Volga cities. An imported quiver with richly ornamented plates of carved bone was found near Samarkand; such plates are well known in the nomadic burials of Mongol times, and were apparently produced for the steppe warriors in the shops of the Golden Horde (Figure 12).

The road from Saraichik to Khwarizm via the Ust-Urt was furnished with caravansaries of a uniform type and constructed at approximately equal distances. As a rule, the buildings were square or rectangular in shape, with a courtyard in the center and rooms around the perimeter. Some of these edifices had covered reservoirs for water. Traveling merchants could rent a room here, leave camels and horses in the care of the guards, place goods in storage, and take a rest beween legs of their journeys. This world of the eastern caravan trade and the caravansaries was a culture all unto itself, one where merchants met, made deals, and exchanged information about conditions and the prices of goods in

Figure 12. Decorated bone plaque for a quiver excavated from a 14th century nomadic grave in the locality of Krivaia Luka. Height 31 cm. (Astrakhan Historic Architectural Museum)

different countries. Long lines of camels trudged along the road from one caravansary to the next, sometimes pulling four-wheeled carriages and wagons. The journey from Sarai to Khwarizm took from forty to forty-five days, although some geographers of the time said that the trip could be completed in twenty-eight days: eight days from Sarai to Saraichik, and twenty from Saraichik to Khwarizm. The journey from Krim to Khwarizm took three months, but the road was safe: in the heyday of the Golden Horde one could travel it without fear or worry, for the central power of the state was still strong enough to ensure safety on the roads.

Although Khwarizmian coins circulated in the European parts of the Golden Horde, they were not very numerous. We know that both trade routes from the Volga area to Khwarizm were intensively used: one through the Ust-Urt and the other through the Mangyshlak peninsula (and further via the Caspian Sea to Hajji-tarkhan in the Volga delta). This would seem to contradict the rarity of Khwarizmian coins in circulation in the Volga region, and likewise the scarcity of coins from the Volga area in Khwarizm. Apparently, this trade made use of a system of written orders and invoices, which was quite well known to eastern traders even in earlier times.

From Khwarizm the road went on to the Far East through Otrar and Almalik. Another route led through Bukhara, Samarkand, and Merv to Iran and India. Trade with Iran was also conducted through the Caucasus: that road went through Derbent and passed the cities of Azerbaijan to Tabriz, the capital of Mongol Iran. Military confrontations between the two empires of the Iranian khanid and the Golden Horde did not usually obstruct trade. Even in the 15th century, when the Golden Horde collapsed and the northern trade route between East and West fell into disuse, trade between Iran and the Volga continued. We know that in 1438 a merchant from Shiraz, one Shams ad-Din Muhammad, traveled with goods to the Volga area and that this trip brought him huge profits. Rather than going through the Caucasus, he chose a route through Central Asia, which was an alternative trade route used when the situation in the Caucasus was particularly dangerous.

Fragments of Iranian pottery are found in the cities of the Golden Horde. Camels and horses were exported from the Golden Horde to Iran, with some herds numbering in the thousands. Merchants brought coins from Iran to the Golden Horde, usually following the khans' military expeditions in Transcaucasia. Hoards are known in which a large percentage of the coins came from Transcaucasian mints. These large collections of foreign coins were quickly dispersed, however, and disappeared among the coins of local origin.

A multilingual dictionary compiled for Golden Horde traders at the end of the 13th century contains, along with Latin and Polovtsian words, columns of Persian ones. A merchant from the Golden Horde had to know, if not the Persian language itself, then at least some key words and important phrases. In fact, the Persian language and its literature were known and appreciated in the Golden Horde. Persian inscriptions can be found there on tiles and bowls, bracelets and other objects (Plates 51, 69, 78, 80, 101, Catalogue Nos. 23, 40, 51, 53, 87). It was customary in Iran to put lines from a famous poet on tiles decorating edifices. One tile from New Sarai bears the following verses from the great Persian poet Sa'adi:

> Oh, heart! Look at the world as you wish. See how people are being afflicted in it, like Noah during the thousand years of his life. See how many gardens and flowers are growing in the world. See how many giant alcazars and palaces there are in the world. See how proudly people robed themselves in thousands of atlases and golden brocades. And then they too were destroyed.

The same verses are found on bowls from the Selitrennoe and Tsarev sites.

From Central Asia the trade routes led to the passes of the Hindukush in Afghanistan, and further into the Indus Valley and deeper into India. We have records of trade in horses with India. On the Tsarev site, a plate was found bearing an open-work depiction of an elephant and a monkey, apparently of Indian craftsmanship. A bronze Buddhist figurine found in the Don basin had an inscription that established the place and time of its making: Nepal 1306. A common find in sites of the Golden Horde epoch are cowrie shells, which served as decorations, and possibly as small change in the system of currency—these shells are found only on the shores of the Indian Ocean.

The most prominent proof of trade connections with India are Indian gold coins, minted by the Sultans of Delhi, which were found in many cities of the Golden Horde. They occur both as individual finds and in hoards (Plates 40-43, Catalogue 18-19). A hoard of silver Khwarizmian coins found in Urgench also contained about a hundred golden dinars. The majority of these were of Indian origin, though several were Egyptian coins, and others were from the mint at Baghdad. This hoard, hidden at the end of the 14th century, reflects the complexity of the trade routes of that era, and the intricate way in which they crossed and intertwined.

A direct steppe route to China began at Saraichik and went through Otrar and Almalik. This road was well guarded: along the road to Almalik, military outposts were situated at one day's journey from each other. The trip from Derbent to China via Sarai took five months. Another route to China, as we have already mentioned, led through Khwarizm. According to Balducci Pegolotti, everyone who intended to bring goods from Venice or Genoa to China had to take textiles with him and go through Urgench to sell them there for silver, after which he could proceed further. One way or the other, merchants of the Golden Horde traveled to China frequently, and often received Chinese traders in their own land, as such trips had long since ceased to be a novelty for the Chinese.

A small hoard of 13th century Chinese coins was found on the Selitrennoe site. Samples of the silks which were now coming from China in large quantities are found in the cemeteries of Golden Horde cities, and in the 14th century burial mounds of wealthy Polovtsy in the steppe. These include silk caftans and shirts, purses, and cases for mirrors. Silk robes were found in the crypt of a rich city dweller on the Uvek site near Saratov, the ruins of the Golden Horde city of Ukek, and a beautiful Chinese silk caftan in a rich female burial of the 14th century near the village of Novo-Pavlovskoe in the Stavropol region. Italian merchants carried silks on to Europe: near Padua in Italy a burial was discovered which was that of a condottiere, wrapped from head to foot in silk, including some most likely of Chinese origin and imported by Italian merchants from the Golden Horde.

Chinese mirrors, as well as their local imitations, are found in Golden Horde cities. There is also much Chinese porcelain with the pale green colored, transluscent glaze called Celadon (Plate 94 left, Catalogue No. 76). Celadon was the name of a western European literary hero, who particularly liked light green ribbons, which is how this type of Chinese pottery got its name in Europe. It is a strange quirk of history that the character himself has been completely forgotten, but his name has become a scientific term describing a special glaze. Other types of Chinese porcelain, with brown or bright blue patterns on a white background, also appear among the ruins of Golden Horde cities. Even porcelain boxes have been unearthed, such as the Chinese used as head supports while sleeping.

This type of porcelain inspired imitations in all the Golden Horde cities. At Selitrennoe, kilns were excavated where glazed bowls of the same pale green color were fired (Plates 91, left; 94, right; Catalogue Nos. 71, 77). These bowls, however, were not of porcelain, but of *kashi*, a distinctive white substance made by mixing sand and clay with glue. Kashi bowls with clear glaze and blue patterns were also fired there, imitating the Chinese porcelain not only in color but also in motifs: lotus flowers, chrysanthemums, bouquets in vases, and dragons Plates 98–100, Catalogue Nos. 83–85). A fragment of a bowl was discovered with a drawing of an arched bridge over a river, executed in the Chinese style, and there are fragments with clouds and birds (Plates 95–97, Catalogue Nos. 78–80). Such ceramics, imitating blue-patterned Chinese porcelain, became very popular and spread all over central Asia and Iran in the 15ᵗʰ century. Scholars call it Timurid because the 15ᵗʰ century was the time when the successors of the formidable conqueror Timur, or Tamerlane, dominated the Middle East. We shall return to Timur himself later, to conclude the history of the cities of the Golden Horde.

Some Chinese ornamental motifs firmly established themselves in Mongol art. The most common among these is known as the "knot of happiness." In the 13th and 14th centuries this decoration appears on clothing, coins, architectural details, and metal objects (Figure 13, Plate 62, Catalogue No. 31).

Iron foundry developed in the Golden Horde cities under the influence of Chinese craftsmen. This technology was known in China from the first millennium B.C.E., whereas in Eastern Europe iron smelting and casting was not in use until the 14ᵗʰ century. The foundries of the Golden Horde produced cauldrons and other items such as bushings for wheels. Archaeologists have found iron-smelting furnaces in Bolgar, one of the cities of the Golden Horde. Most metal articles, however, were forged from the metal ore after heating it to a high temperature, but not to the smelting point, which was too high for ancient craftsmen to attain.

Figure 13. Golden bracelet with "knot of happiness," Selitrennoe. Length 19 cm, Width O.9 centimeter.

As early as the 13th century, silver vessels—bowls and vases—started flowing from China to the Mongol-dominated Eurasian steppe. In the Mongol leaders' headquarters and in the cities, local craftsmen copied these models for their patrons, gradually departing further and further from the original patterns. This led to the local production of silver and golden bowls and other toreutic ware in which traces of Chinese art are clearly visible: paired fish (a widespread Chinese Buddhist symbol), lotus flowers, and clouds. The lotus was especially

Figure 14. Gold vessel with handles in the shape of dolphins, Tsarevskoe site. Height 13 c. (State Hermitage, Saint Petersburg)

popular. In the Golden Horde it appears everywhere—on majolica tiles, decorating city buildings, on pottery, and on objects made of precious metals (Plates 87, 88, 97, Catalogue Nos. 61–64, 80–82). It appears on the well known regalia of the Russian tsars, the so called "Crown of Monomakhos," which has been shown to be a product of Central Asian and Golden Horde workmanship of the 14th century, given to a Russian prince by a Tatar ruler. A golden bowl with handles in the shape of dolphins in the Chinese style was found at Tsarev (Figure 14); a number of vessels of this type have been found in the steppe area. From the burial of Gashun-Ust in the northern Caucasus come silver buckles depicting deer under a tree; their exact counterparts can be found in the art of the Jurchen, a Far Eastern people conquered by Genghiz

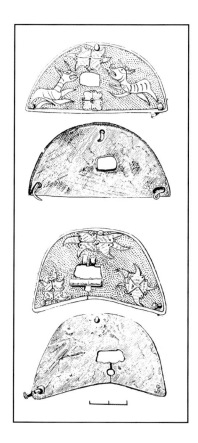

Figure 15. Silver plaques found near Volgograd. Length 8.1 cm. (Volgograd Museum of Local Lore)

Khan. A chance find near Volgograd of two silver plaques adorned with animals and ornamental patterns gives an example of Golden Horde workmanship deeply influenced by Chinese art (Figure 15). A set of gilded bronze belt decorations with buckles and plaques executed in the Chinese style was found at Selitrennoe (Plate 64, Catalogue No. 34).

Chinese mirrors and imitations of them are quite common finds on the sites of the Golden Horde period and in the burial mounds of the surrounding no-madic peoples (Figure 16).

If we could enter an ordinary Golden Horde home, we would certainly find there a warmed bench, heated by a horizontal flue coming from the stove: an appliance with its origins in the Chinese heating system known as *kan* (Plates 4–8). One of the houses excavated on the Tsarev site, the ruins of New Sarai, had walls made of wooden panels. In the center of the building there was a heated room with a kan, surrounded by an unheated corridor. The construction of this house apparently followed Chinese building practices.

Figure 16. Bronze mirror from Selitennoe. Length 8.6 cm. (Astrakhan Historic Architectural Museum)

Chinese elements in the culture of the Golden Horde were combined randomly with decorative elements borrowed from Byzantium, Iran, Central Asia, Volga Bulgaria, the Crimea, and the Caucasus, giving rise to hybrid objects with mixed styles. One of the most distinctive examples of this eclectic style has already been mentioned: the Crown of Monomakhos. Executed using the widespread filigree technique, it was decorated with Chinese lotuses while at the same time showing elements of Byzantine design. Another example is a silver goblet from the Belorechenskaia burial mounds. Although it was produced by Golden Horde craftsmen, their typical style was combined with features borrowed from Arabic silversmiths in Iran and Mesopotamia, such as the figure of a bird on the goblet's open-work interior (Figure 17). These and many other examples show that different artistic styles and traditions were merging during this period of intensive contacts between East and West. Elements of Far and Near Eastern culture percolated through the Golden Horde even as far as the "Russian ulus," that is, the culture of medieval Russia. A Russian chronicle mentions a Central Asian people, the Tangut, and Old Russian calendars reflected the Far Eastern "animal" cycle of years.

Thus, the Mongol empire and after them, the Golden Horde, was a bridge connecting Asia and Europe. The northern routes of the Great Silk Road became the most important of the time, and in the long dialogue between East and West, the cities of the Golden Horde were destined to speak with a loud and important voice.

Figure 17. Silver goblet from the Belorechenskie barrows. Height 13 cm. (State Hermitage, Saint Petersburg)

Chapter 6
Money

International trade and exchange with distant countries as well as internal trade was developed during the time of the Golden Horde. In its noisy, crowded city markets, a brisk barter economy went on. Large and small weights, a distinctive characteristic of market trade, are found in the Golden Horde sites (Plate 107, Catalogue Nos. 103, 106, 107). And what is trade without money and coins? There were silver coins, called dirhams, and copper ones, puls. Golden dinars were struck in Khwarizm.

Golden Horde coinage is so abundant as to pose a challenge to the best of Russian orientalists. Near the village of Karachun in Tatarstan, a hoard of Golden Horde silver coins was discovered which weighed 34 kilograms, and comprised about 28,000 specimens—it took the author 10 years to compile a full card index of this hoard (Figure 18, Plate 39, Catalogue No. 17). Another hoard, also discovered in Tatarstan, contained some 20,000 silver coins and several golden dinars of Indian origin. The total number of recorded hordes of the Golden Horde coins is nearly half a thousand, including several in Russia—in the regions of Ryazan and Nizhniy Novgorod, and along the upper Don and the northern Donets and Oka—as well as in the Ukraine, Moldova, and Romania, not to mention the lands of the Golden Horde proper in the Volga region, and in Volga Bulgaria, the Crimea, and the northern Caucasus.

Some of these hoards are especially interesting and reveal family history, such as one discovered in Feodosiya in 1898, comprised of silver coins of the khans of the Golden Horde and those of the Girei Dynasty, the Crimean offspring of the Jöchi family. The coins were in a large ceramic jar, with another, smaller jar inside it, and were divided into four portions. It is clear that these jars were not filled with coins all at once: four generations of dedicated collectors had amassed this treasure, which the family's last representative consigned to the earth. He put the jar into a pit and covered it with soil, after ordering an inscription to be written:

> The earth kept the basis for my great-grandfather, who served Toqtamish, and he gave it to his son Yahya ibn Mansur ibn Yusuf Tarakhgi, and the son of my great-grandfather served Timur-Qutlugh, the Great Sultan, and he increased it and tripled many of the things which he had inherited, and gave them to his son Iblan b. Yahya b. Mansur b. Yusuf Tarakhgi, who was faithful to his master, the Great Mengli Girei b. Hajji-Girei b. Ghiyath ad-Din of the glorious descendants of Jöchi, and he rewarded me and gave it to me, and I have served the Great Sultan, the Just Khan, now deceased, Salamat Girei.

Thus we are presented with the hoard's entire history: the great-grandfather of its last owner had served Toqtamish, Khan of the Golden Horde from 1380 to 1400. His money fitted into the first small jar, filling just half of it. Then his son filled this small jar to the top with his own coins, which he had accumulated in the service of another khan, Timur Qutlugh (1397–1399). Before putting them in the jar, he wrapped his savings in a piece of cloth. Then this jar came into the possession of the grandson, who served the Crimean khan Mengli Girei (1469–1515). This man put the small jar inside the larger one and filled half of the empty space between the jars with his own coins. Finally, the great-grandson, the treasure's last owner, who worked at the court of Khan Salamat Girei (1608–1610), filled the remainder of the large jar and had the inscription written. At the end of the inscription we read:

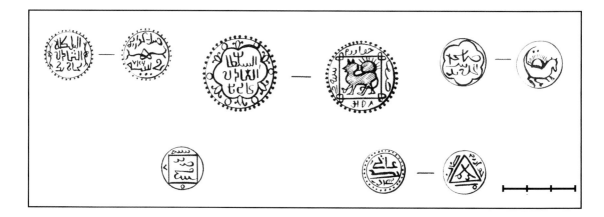

Figure 18. Golden Horde coins. Selitrennoe. Maximum diameter 2 cm. (Astrakhan Historic

No children of mine are with me, wives and kinsmen, strength of my sons, children of youth [are not with me]. They are killed and I am alone, infirm and helpless as a child who has left his mother's womb. Oh grief, oh sorrow, tears and sobbing over the ashes of the young. I search hopelessly for medicine. Now in the month of Rabi the First of the year 1019 [in the Islamic reckoning; 1610 C.E.], without hesitation I give this last handful of wealth to the people of prayer for writing books, so that they can spend it exclusively to teach the ignorant and to enlighten the unlearned.

Among the last portion of coins was a rich belt bearing the inscription "The Just Sultan Salamat Girei." Evidently this was a gift from the patron to the last owner of the treasure. There were also earlier gifts of similar kind made to other members of this family, for example, a buckle bearing the name of Toqtamish. Luxurious utensils and armor accompanied the coins, and there was even a stump of a finger with a precious ring. The last of this miserly line, however, never managed to give his money to the "people of prayer"—he buried the family savings in the ground. Apparently, he found it easier to die this way.

Such hoards are our major source of information about coinage and monetary circulation. The first genuine Jöchid coinage was minted in the 1260s, issued by Khan Mangu Timur and signals his formal separation from the ulus of the great khan. The first coins were minted in the cities of Volga Bulgaria, while another center of monetary production was the Crimea. Beginning in the 1270s, coinage starts in Sarai and Khwarizm, and then in Azaq and Ukek. The primary metal used for Golden Horde coinage was silver, which came as tribute from the conquered lands of Russia. This draining of silver out of Russia so exhausted the country's resources that Russia was unable to restart its own coinage until late in the 14th century.

Reforms intended to unify coinage were undertaken during the reign of Khan Toqtai in 1310, and local minting of silver was practically abolished. Instead, a silver coin—a dirham of a standard weight—started being minted in Sarai. These abundant dirhams from Sarai forced nearly all other coins out of circulation in the markets of most of the Golden Horde provinces. Beginning in the 1340s, the mint at New Sarai (Sarai al-Jadid) began issuing coins, and in the 1350s it was joined by Gulistan, a Golden Horde city whose exact location still remains a mystery. These mints were the major providers of coins to all the outlying regions of the Golden Horde up to 1360s. The weight of their coins was very stable and remained practically unchanged until the 1370s.

The weight of dirhams, however, was still checked during payments, using a small scale made of bone, specially designed for this purpose. It had a small spade-shaped widening on one end of the balance, and a counterweight on the other. One had simply to pick the coin up with this "spade" and, by observing the weight it would be obvious if the specimen were counterfeit, or if it had had its edges trimmed.

From the 1360s, intensive minting started in Azaq, and then in the mobile capital of Orda. The coins of Azaq and Orda followed local standards, different from the weight norms of the coins from Sarai, Sarai al-Jadid, and Gulistan, thus putting an end to the domination of the stable dirham minted to a common standard. As scholars observe, from that moment on the so called "numismatic provinces" emerged, where circulation was dominated by local coins. The coinage from the mints in the Volga region became depleted and apparently unable to supply the markets of other regions with silver coins, and the Golden Horde suffered a production crisis. In the 1370s the markets experienced a severe shortage of silver coins.

In 1381 Khan Toqtamish conducted a new monetary reform, aimed at unifying and improving the system of currency. All the centers that were by that time minting coins (Sarai, New Sarai, Azaq, Krim, Hajji-tarkhan, and Majar) were obliged to use the same weight standard. This reform was fully enforced, however, only in the Volga region, where the capitals were located. In other areas the old coins continued to circulate alongside the new ones, in a ratio established by the markets.

A third attempt at state monetary reform took place in the Golden Horde during the rule of Edigei in 1400, but it too failed to bring unity to the currency. With each new reform, the Khan's treasury received new income at the expense of the population—old dirhams were outlawed, taken out of circulation, and exchanged for new ones on the basis of an exchange rate which was, of course, profitable for the state, and disadvantageous for the population.

There was a practice of "open" or "free" production of silver coins at the request of honest people who brought silver to a mint. These individuals would receive a specified number of coins of known weight and purity in exchange for a specified amount of metal submitted; some coins were retained by the mint as payment for the work and as a treasury fee. The khan's financial advisors were well aware of the currency laws, and the authorities of the Golden Horde "adjusted" the currency by constant renewal of the copper circulation and issuance of new copper puls.

The right to mint coins belonged exclusively to the khans of the Jöchid family, the descendants of Jöchi, who was the eldest son of Genghiz Khan. Even such all-powerful military commanders and ruling emirs as Mamay and Edigei could not issue coins in their own name, because they were not Jöchids. The coins of the 13th century and of the provincial towns in the first quarter of the 14th century bear the Jöchid imperial seal, or tamga, as a symbol of the unity of the ruling family, and also to claim the state as the sole property of the Jöchid family. The khan's name, an indication of the mint, and year of issue are nearly always present on silver coins of the 14th century. In that century, anonymous issues of silver and golden coins were always the result of the appearance of separatist tendencies in certain regions. One example of such coinage comes from Khwarizm in the 1360s and 1370s, where representatives of the semiautonomous dynasty of local rulers were afraid to mint coins bearing their own names—the prerogative of the khans—and so issued coins without any name, merely indicating that these were coins of Khwarizm.

The name of a khan appears rarely on copper coins. Many copper issues have a legend fixing the a ratio between silver dirhams and copper puls. Normally, the name of the mint and the date were indicated, but many types are lacking this information. Often various pictorial images were placed on copper coins: birds, animals, and bows and arrows; they occur on dirhams only in the 13th century. Puls of the 14th century often carry astrological signs—a lion and the sun, the sun in Cancer's claws, Aquarius, and Libra. Occasionally there are representations of beasts of prey, camels, horsemen, a building with a crescent, two donkeys by a trough, a bird, one or two fishes, a peacock with tail spread, a rosette, a poleaxe, a woman with a child, or a double-headed eagle, but whatever special meaning these figures may have had remains unknown. In addition to silver and copper coins, bar-shaped silver ingots weighing 195–197 grams, called sum, were also used in trade.

Monetary hoards can tell us about coinage, currency, and reforms. We come across the small savings of poor people and huge treasures left by the wealthy. As especially numerous finds are usually encountered along roads, coin hordes are indicators of the location of ancient roads. There are also hoards consisting of both luxury objects and coins. We turn now to a discussion of one of these.

Chapter 7

The Simferopol Treasure

It is possible to spend years excavating the remains of a major ancient kingdom's capital and find no precious materials, so that even a couple of golden plaques can be seen as a blessing. Meanwhile, someone who has no connection to archaeology gets lucky: the quirks of fate let him stumble on a collection of rich and precious objects. Something sparkles under a spade or a bulldozer's blade, and turns out to be an ancient treasure. This happened in 1967, in the Crimean city of Simferopol, where a large hoard of precious objects from the Golden Horde epoch was discovered.

The eclectic nature of the Golden Horde culture becomes obvious to anyone who has ever had a chance to hold items from this treasure trove in his hands. The typical style of Central Asian and Iranian art and craft, the influence of Italian art, and the traditional elements of Far Eastern ornamentation are easily recognizable. The diversity of decorations is combined with the special splendor that marks jewelry of that time. Filigree and granulation are the main techniques. Forms are complex and intricate, and every turn creates a new interplay of lines, of hundreds of tiny beads and microthreads.

The mere list of objects in the Simferopol treasure boggles the mind. These were the belongings of a rich aristocrat, possibly one of the Jöchid family, and included a p'ai-tzü—a "tablet of authority" bearing the name of Khan Keldibeg (Plates 56, 57, Catalogue No. 28), a bowl with magical inscriptions (Plates 58, 59, Catalogue No. 29), silver spoons, and a ladle with the figure of a man in a pointed cap holding a vessel to his mouth (Plates 60, 61, Catalogue No. 30). There were also golden dinars issued by the Sultans of Delhi, dating to the late 13th and mid-14th century (Plates 40–43, Catalogue

Nos. 18, 19), and coin-shaped golden pendants. There are belts with buckles and plaques decorated in the Italian style, most likely brought from Italian cities (Plates 44–48, Catalogue Nos. 20, 21).

There are many other belt decorations produced by the jewelers of the Golden Horde. We must not forget that a belt was not only an article of clothing and a decoration—it also served to indicate its wearer's social rank. One set of golden belt ornaments consisted of a tongue, a plaque with a hook, two plaques with shackles for hanging objects, and rectangular or heart-shaped scalloped plaques and frames. They had framed carnelian and were decorated with golden open-work plaques with figured grapevines, and silver plaques mounted beneath them as a background. Altogether this set consisted of 31 objects (Plates 49, 50, Catalogue No. 22).

The details of a woman's gold headpiece are especially splendid. The set comprised 19 plaques and finials inlaid with pearls and precious stones—sapphires, emeralds, amethysts, turquoise, jasper, and olivine. The second finial of the Simferopol treasure is made up of silver items and is decorated with pearls. Smaller objects include golden earrings and plaques decorated in the filigree technique with pearls and stones of various colors (Plates 54, 55, Catalogue Nos. 26, 27), carnelian beads, sapphires, and button-pendants of crystal and gold.

Golden bracelets with niello and filigree work would delight anyone who saw them. One of these bracelets has a Persian inscription: "Let the Creator of the World be a protector of the owner of this, wherever he goes" (Plate 51, Catalogue No. 23). Another type of golden bracelet is bent from a rod, circular in section, and decorated with animal heads at each end (Plate 52, Catalogue No. 24). There are also intricate chains—probably part of the headgear—made up of individual plaques with granulation work and studded with turquoise, pearls, and spinels (Plate 53, Catalogue No. 25). The rich and diverse abundance of this treasure also included golden cases for paper amulets, spells and texts from the Qur'an; these too were adorned with granulation and inset colored stones (Plates 62, 63, Catalogue Nos. 31–33).

The objects from the Simferopol treasure are typical representatives of the decorative art of the Golden Horde, as well as of the contemporary art of Central Asia, brimming with decorative elements and the luxuriant flourishing of forms and ornaments that is the splendid imperial gala style, characteristic of the art of great powers.

Chapter 8
The Archaeology of New Sarai

As it happened, the second capital of the Golden Horde became an object of study long before the ruins of the first one provoked any serious interest among archaeologists. The Tsarev site, beneath which the ruins of New Sarai (Sarai al-Jadid) were hidden, began to attract attention as early as the 19th century, and the history of excavations on this monument turned out to be long and highly tempestuous.

"No special knowledge is required from the officer whose responsibility is to supervise the opening of the aforementioned mounds and banks, but only the collection and delivery of all the necessary objects, while a special order will be issued later concerning a scholarly exploration of these," wrote L. A. Perovskiy, the Minister of Interior Affairs, in his circular of 1843 regarding the organization of excavations at the Sarai-Tsarev site. A. V. Tereshchenko, who was sent to do the actual work on the site, was not, however, merely an officer suited only for "collecting objects." He was also a scholar. Considering that at that time the science of archaeology did not exist at all, we can consider Tereshchenko's explorations as among the earliest archaeological excavations in Russia.

To begin with, Tereshchenko decided to make a topographic map of the ruins. Leaving nothing to guesswork or chance, he instructed the topographers to mark on the map only those remains which were visible, that is, the parts of ancient buildings that remained above the surface of the site. Although the method of excavation was primitive, Tereshchenko described all the structural remains that his workers' spades uncovered. He indicated the areas of his excavation on the map, and supplemented this with drawings and sketches.

Unfortunately, Tereshchenko was unable to carry his style of work through to the end of his explorations. The authorities, contemptuous of his attempt at a scholarly approach to the study of the ruins of the Golden Horde capital, demanded that he come up with sensational finds. The following year Tereshchenko hired many more workers. They went through and hurriedly dug up everything, not taking the time to do more than pull the ancient artifacts out of the ground. At first, Tereshchenko attempted to give some description of the structures they uncovered, but in the following years he ceased even these cursory attempts. The finds were collected in one great heap and sent that way to Saint Petersburg, accompanied only by a brief inventory. Tereshchenko's journals became more and more terse; his drawings and sketches rarer and rarer. As the scope of the excavations grew from year to year, the excavation techniques went from bad to worse. Tereshchenko, who had started as a scholar, ended up as a treasure-hunter. During the last years of his work in Tsarev he was interested only in beautiful and luxurious objects. His excavations lasted nine years in all, from 1843 until 1851.

During this time a huge bulk of material was uncovered, pouring out as if from a cornucopia. Each turn of the spade brought up some fragment or remnant of past times. "In one small square area," Tereshchenko wrote,

> . . . strewn with small fragments of brick, there lay in great abundance broken colored and glass tableware, bowls, ink-pots, pieces of leather, leather cut out for high boots and shoes, canvas, silk textiles, and clothing—all burnt; knives, sword blades, axes, spades, frying pans, basins used for ritual washing, pokers, tinder, steel for kindling fire, small knives, cast iron cauldrons, copper bowls, copper goblets, copper candlesticks, knitting needles, fragments of scissors, necklaces, burned paper, small knives, birch bark, burned woven mats, nails, hooks, door hinges, locks and padlocks, pieces of burned baked bread, rye, wheat, walnuts and hazelnuts, nutgalls, acorns, almonds, raisins, plums, grapes, peaches, pistachios, rosemary, pepper, and beans . . . . Pieces of crystal, dyes of blue, yellow, light blue, green, red, and white, rings from horse-collars and bridles, bits, chains, iron horseshoes, iron bushings for wheels, resin, sheets of copper, whetstones, slates, stones for grinding dyes, clay skittles, balls, copper wire, hoes, sulfur, alum, saltpeter, and millet were discovered in heaps in the three stone vaults on this spot. The diversity of the objects discovered in this one place allows us to suggest that this was a bazaar, with a built-in stone storage container inside it for the merchandise, of the sort which exists in nearly every Asiatic city.

In 1959 the Volga Regional Archaeological Expedition, under the direction of the author, began a new round, this time aiming at a systematic scholarly excavation of the Tsarev site. We discovered numerous lower- and middle-class houses: dugouts, dwellings partially sunk into the ground, houses with wooden walls on brick socles, and single- and multi-room dwellings built of mud bricks and baked bricks. These structures show a whole hierarchy of habitations, from those of the poorest to those of the richest inhabitants. Let us begin at the very bottom of the social structure.

Chapter 9
The Lower Classes

Johannes de Piano Carpini wrote that when the Mongols are standing in front of the fortress, they speak to the besieged politely and make many promises in order to make them surrender; they say to those who surrender: "Come out so that we can count you, according to our custom." Then when they come out to them, they ask who among them are craftsmen and they retain those; they decapitate the others with an axe, except for those whom they want to keep as slaves. If they spare some of the others, as it was said, there are never noble or authoritative people among them. But if for some particular reason they retain noble people, they are unable to free themselves from captivity, neither by appeals nor by the payment of a ransom.

A craftsman turned slave was a typical representative of the Golden Horde's population, forcibly brought by the Mongols from a destroyed city, the images of the destruction and death of his home and family still fresh in his memory. He would remember how, for many long years, he had been driven from place to place among the mass of captives, forced to follow the Mongol troops, to perform the dirtiest and hardest jobs for the army, to be the first to cross dangerous rivers, testing fords, stepping into unpredictable swamps. He would remember it well despite the decades that might have passed since his captivity and enslavement. His life had been spared only because he was an excellent craftsman, and now in this new life he and his children were destined to work for their enslavers.

Such enslaved craftsmen, from Central Asia and Transcaucasia, Iran and the Crimea, Russia and Volga Bulgaria were numerous in the cities of the Golden Horde. Craftsmen from Central Asia decorated palaces and mosques with tiles and carved stucco, and produced glazed pottery. There were smiths and bronze-founders, weavers and stonemasons among the slaves. Coiners brought to Sarai from Khwarizm organized the minting of dirhams, which originally followed the Khwarizmian patterns. These people defined the appearance of the new cities and the eclectic character of the Golden Horde culture.

Slave-craftsmen worked in large workshops belonging to the Mongol nobility. In Iran such a shop was called a *karkhanah*, that is "room" or "place" of work. Throughout the day, the slaves of rich noblemen were worked to the bone in the karkhanah, and at night they were taken to large dugouts. They were lucky if the dugout had a stove and benches. Even some of these slave quarters had no stoves, so that in winter there was no heat. The slaves would be given a charcoal brazier, the only source of heat for twenty to thirty people, locked in these pits in the ground through the long winter nights. To prevent the digging of escape tunnels, the walls of dugouts were often lined with fired bricks; armed guards watched over the entrances.

Piano Carpini describes the slaves' meager rations: "They give to each one daily a small weight of meal, and nothing else but a little portion of meat three times a week." He also mentions that the slightest sign of disobedience was punished by beatings as if these were not people, but donkeys. They were shabbily clad: sometimes their only outfits were fur pants for both the intense heat of the steppe summer and the bitterly cold winter of these regions. Slaves often died from cold, or lost fingers and toes to frostbite.

But even such wretched souls as these had hope. The feudal system was taking over. Slavery, which had flourished during the time of the Mongol conquests, became an anachronism by the 14th century. Life itself, and the economy, forced the Mongol aristocrats and khans to free some of their slaves and to turn them into clients—city dwellers liable for both state taxes and duties, which were paid to their masters. A good craftsman could buy himself at least partial freedom after decades of saving any money which he might receive now and then. Jewelers, especially goldsmiths, could earn more as independent craftsmen, and an owner of such slaves benefited by freeing them, on the constant payment of a large duty. Piano Carpini mentions, however, that some slaves had bad owners who did not allow them to work on the side; these slaves had to work so hard that they had no time to earn anything for themselves. Some slaves did become freedmen, building up their own families and households and turning into city folk dependent on the upper social classes. These could save a little for themselves, and had some personal interest in the results of their work.

Our excavations at New Sarai also explored rich buildings, containing golden objects, silver jewelry with turquoise inlay, and beautiful tableware. Next to these aristocratic houses we discovered large dugouts without stoves, probably intended as "barracks" for the slaves of the house's aristocratic owner. Slightly further away, we excavated small dugouts with stoves. These latter were unlikely to belong to free independent city dwellers, who preferred to live in "surface" buildings; they were more likely to be the homes of former slaves who were allowed to have their own households. The owner would not permit them to move away completely, and continued to keep them under tight control. The surface houses of brick which appeared between these dugouts were possibly those of guards.

The dugout became a symbol of slave status, and those who managed to free themselves from the immediate dependence on their owners were eager to move from dugouts to "surface" buildings. Brick houses were the privilege of the upper classes. Poor people usually built houses of wood, but they were "surface" ones. One of our excavation trenches revealed several dugouts, belonging to the early period of habitation on this site, probably the time when large numbers of slaves had been driven there and were erecting the new capital for the khan. After some time had passed, these slaves started gaining their freedom as city commoners. Dugouts were replaced by wooden-walled houses, only partially sunk into the soil.

One of these houses had a large stove and a special oven for baking flat bread. This house was fenced and had its own yard with storage pits for grain and dried fish, a small canopy, open fireplaces, and so on. Originally the entire area had consisted of randomly placed dugouts for dependent builders, but later this quarter was organized into blocks, divided by streets. The owner of this comfortable and roomy house may have been irritated by one feature of his dwelling, which might have reminded him of his past as a slave: the structure was partially sunk into the ground—it was practically a dugout. The owner had then filled in the dugout and built, in its place, a new surface house with a brick floor and walls of wooden logs.

Some freedmen became well-to-do individuals, and were sometimes even able to exert a certain degree of influence at the khan's court or in a nobleman's manor. In

Mongolia, William of Rubruck met a certain Paquette, a French woman from Metz in Lorraine, who had been captured in Hungary. This woman preserved some of her Gallic vivaciousness, in spite of all the horrible suffering and humiliation that she had been through. In time, however, her life had settled down: she had married a Russian and had three beautiful boys. She held a prominent position at the court of a Mongol princess, while her husband was a builder and made good money, although he had once been a slave too, seized in Russia by Batu's troops. In Karakorum, Rubruck found a Parisian goldsmith, William Buchier. He may have been taken to the Mongol capital as a slave, but had managed to stand out because of his skills and artistic taste. Khan Möngke had charged Buchier with the extremely important work of creating a splendid throne for him, and provided him with three thousand marks and fifty helpers. Not everyone, however, turned out to be so lucky. Most captives remained in slavery to the end of their days, and only their children could hope for freedom, albeit a partial one.

Russian princes often found compatriots in Orda or Sarai, where they were obliged to go to express allegiance to the khan of the Golden Horde, or to petition a *yarliq*, or imperial edict allowing them to rule or to settle some dynastic feud. Some of these Russians had ended up here as captives turned into slaves, and later their children or grandchildren gained their freedom and lived in separate colonies within the capital of the Golden Horde. In the archaeological excavations in Golden Horde town sites, numerous pendant crosses and small icons were found, which had belonged to orthodox Christians who had held onto their faith in the Muslim city (Figure 19). The Volga expedition discovered a whole quarter full of Russian pottery and Orthodox crosses in the ruins of a small Golden Horde city now known as Vodiansk, near the regional center of Dubovka in the Volgograd oblast.

Figure 19. Bronze icon with an image of St. George, found in the village of Moshaik, near Astrakhan. Height 7.4 cm. (Astrakhan Historic Architectural Museum)

66

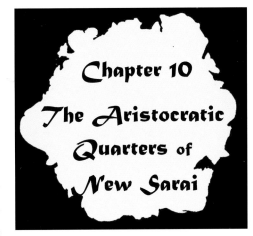

Chapter 10
The Aristocratic Quarters of New Sarai

The eastern and southeastern sections of New Sarai (Tsarev) were occupied by the manors and palaces of the Golden Horde aristocracy. A traveler coming from the east would encounter the palaces of the Mongol nobility while still on the far approaches to the city. Soon, amid the press of merchants, craftsmen, and peasants, he would find himself in a narrow passageway between the manors, which seemed to oversee all those who entered the city beneath their gaze. Finally, the traveler would come to a large square, beyond which the city itself began. Here there were four huge reservoirs, where one could unload goods and water horses, camels, and donkeys. To the north and west of the square were areas of poor houses, winding streets, and ditches full of dirty water; to the south lay the aristocratic quarters.

Each compound consisted of one wealthy manor (Figure 20), fenced in by an earthen wall, which also enclosed a reservoir that supplied the manor with water. The central part was occupied by several buildings, dwellings for the head of the household and his family. There were often two absolutely identical houses symmetrical to one another, one of them being used perhaps by the male side of the family, while the other was reserved for the female household members. These main buildings were surrounded by various ancillary structures: stables, summer kitchens, raised platforms under canopies, and the like.

In the course of time, however, the cloistered character of the aristocratic dwellings changed: our expedition excavated several manors with adjoining houses that belonged to poor people who depended in some way on the owner of the manor. It is worth

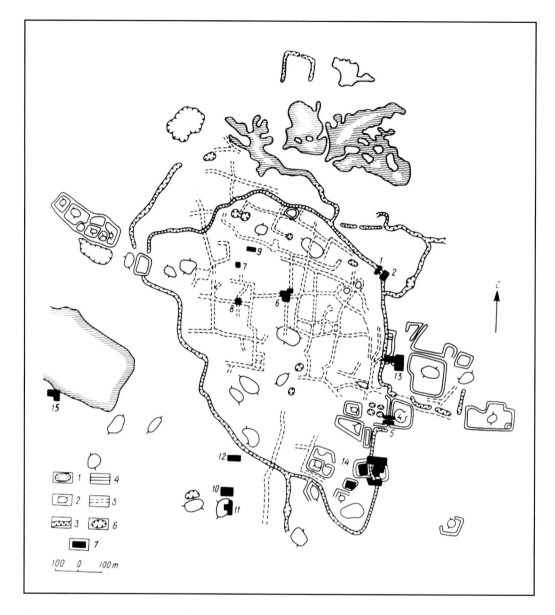

Figure 20. Plan of the Tsarev (New Sarai): 1—lake; 2—hillocks formed by the ruins of houses; 3—moats and ramparts; 4—fences of manors; 5—streets; 6—pits and reservoirs; 7—excavation sites

noting that in several manors, houses were built on a single, systematic plan. They were erected, apparently, following instructions received from the manor's owner, in accordance with his vision of the building, and appear to have been meant as dwellings of dependents and servants, freedmen or pauperized vassals, who had been forced to move to their lord's household, or craftsmen who had sold themselves into bondage. These manors included small craft shops; traces of pottery production were found in one, and in another the dwelling of a goldsmith and the home of a bone-carver.

The Mongol nobility had once lived a nomadic life. An aristocrat would look down on a city dweller, unable to understand how people could vegetate in stuffy cities and take up degrading trades or crafts, when the open steppe lay all around them, roamed by herds of horses, and when there were vast conquered and yet unconquered lands where one could amuse himself by robbing others. But times change. What could one do with trunks full of treasure, with mountains of rich textiles and colorful silks, silver ingots and golden bowls, and crowds of beautiful girls and strong men? They had to be sold, and then the money had to be spent somehow. The Mongol nomadic freebooters became more and more friendly with the city's leadership. These Mongols settled in the cities, forming partnerships with rich merchants and creating large factories which employed enslaved captives. Some of the Mongol nomads left the steppe for a new life, that of pious, quiet, and thrifty citizens, or sedate courtiers of the khan's palace, or wily diplomats, or pilfering bureaucrats.

Yet memories of the old nomadic life lasted long. During the excavation of one rich manor, remains of gers were found: circles of broken bricks used around the edges of their portable housing. The manor's owner had an excellent brick house, but in the summer—perhaps in order to feel like a nomad again—he preferred to move into a yurt that stood permanently on his grounds.

Still, the question asked by nearly every expedition to visit the site was, "Where is the khan's palace?" No one can resist the urge to ask: "So, did you finally find the palace of Khan Özbeg?"

Where, indeed, was the khan's palace? It had to be somewhere, of course—did Tereshchenko find it? He wrote nothing about this, but let us look at what he sent from Tsarev. We see before us a mass of mosaics and tiles, some of them lustre-glazed so that they appeared gilted. Splendid patterns in blue, turquoise, and ultramarine, the white letters of inscriptions in Arabic, yellow and red flowers. And what kind of tableware did Tereshchenko dig up? There are intact bowls now in the Hermitage collection, covered with a colorful glazing and delicate patterns—birds and animals, stars and rosettes, and decorated with "woven" ornaments and scrolls. It is hard to believe that such splendid glazed and gilded vessels as Tereshchenko found could have belonged to a mere commoner.

We did also find fine objects like these during our excavations of rich houses that were not the royal quarters. A large silver dish with an inscription in the Kipchak language, recording the weight of silver it contained, must also be from a rich house. That is definitely the case with another dish, also with an inscription, although this time in Russian: "And this is the chalice of Prince Volodimir, son of David, and the one who drinks from it, let him be healthy, and the praise be to God and to our Lord the Grand Prince." This princely treasure was seized by the Mongols when they stormed and looted the city of Chernigov. After journeying long in the trains of Batu's army, this dish came to Sarai, where it was finally found by a Russian archaeologist.

Among all these items, a splendid golden cup found by Tereshchenko in 1848 stands out. We have seen this vessel already in our discussion of trade (Figure 14) two dolphins are depicted on its handles and its weight is 850 grams. It was found by accident in an area that had been already excavated; the workers had missed it the first time. But something made Tereshchenko ask for this place to be checked once more, just in case. Tereshchenko was so pleased with this find that he nominated the man responsible for it for an incentive medal. Interestingly, the same worker soon outdid himself again by finding a hoard of silver ingots.

It is still unclear as to exactly where all these things were found. Did Tereshchenko and his workers in fact excavate the royal quarters? It is hard to say now, but it is possible. Tereshchenko explored nearly every large hill in the area of Tsarev. Will we one day find the palace, or any traces remaining of it after the excavations of the 1840s and 1850s? Even these remains would be interesting, as Tereshchenko left us neither plans nor any description of the buildings, so any new discoveries would allow us to understand at least what kind of palace it had been.

Chapter 11

The Excavations in Old Sarai

The age of the Golden Horde is one of the Russian people's worst historical memories. It is not only the destruction and pillaging, the servility of Russian princes to their new lords, and the death of hundreds of thousands that accounts for the bitter memory of these times. The Russian people were scattered across the steppe of the huge Eurasian continent, to pine away in Tatar captivity on the banks of the Volga, or in the Kipchak steppe or far-off Mongolia. (Old) Sarai, the capital of the Golden Horde, remained an accursed, hated place in the Russian memory, a place where everything was alien and hostile for Russians—as it was for many other conquered peoples as well.

For the khans of the Golden Horde, the tears and blood of Russians, Bulgarians, people from the Caucasus and Central Asia, and craftsmen from the Crimea and China created splendid cities, which were like beautiful flowers that blossomed and then quickly faded away. When the famous Arab traveler Ibn Battuta visited these cities and looked at them without animosity or hatred, he was struck by their richness, splendor, and energy:

> The city of al-Sara is one of the finest of cities, of boundless size, situated in a plain, choked with the throng of its inhabitants, and possessing good bazaars and broad streets. We rode out one day with one of its principal men, intending to make a circuit of the city and find out its extent. Our lodging place was at one end of it and we set out from it in the early morning, and it was after midday when we reached the other end. . . This too through a continuous line of houses, among which there were no ruins and no gardens. The city has thirteen mosques for the holding of Friday prayers. . . . As for the other mosques, they are exeedingly numerous. There are various groups of people among its inhabitants; these

include the Mongols, who are the dwellers in this country and its sultans, and some of whom are Muslims, then the As, who are Muslims, the Kipchak, the Cherkess, the Rus, and the Rum—[all of] these are Christians. Each group lives in a separate quarter with its own bazaars. Merchants and strangers from the two Iraqs, Egypt, Syria and elsewhere, live in a quarter which is surrounded by a wall for the protection of the properties of the merchants.

Another 14th century Arab writer, al-Omari, recorded the words of merchants who returned from the Golden Horde:

> The city of Sarai stands on salt-marsh land without any fortifications. The khan's residence is a large palace, surmounted with a golden crescent. The palace is surrounded by the walls, towers, and houses, where the khan's emirs live. Their winter quarters are in this palace. This river Edil-Volga is three times larger than the Nile, or even larger, and large ships navigate it and go to the Russians and Slavs. The source of this river is also in the land of the Slavs. The city is huge and has markets, baths, and religious buildings, as well as places for the storage of arriving goods.

In the first quarter of the 14th century, Old Sarai was indeed a large city with mosques and palaces, crowded bazaars, and warehouses for merchandise. It was a city where one could meet foreign merchants and scholars, and see people of different lands, dressed in

Figure 21. Fragments of alabaster panel with the depiction of running animals, Selitrennoe. Width 8 cm. (Astrakhan Historic Architectural Museum)

their national clothing, speaking various languages, and worshiping different gods. What is left of this city? Fragments of the past buried in the soil, burnt by the sun and washed over by rain, flat hills preserving the ruins of houses that once boasted splendid colorful tiles (Plates 67–81, Catalogue Nos. 37–54), carved stucco, and terra-cotta (Figures 21–23). Of the basins once filled with cool water, only holes in the ground remain.

And there are, of course, memories. This is the site of the ancient capital, a huge archaeological dig near the village of Selitrennoe on the Akhtuba, along the lower Volga. In 1972, the Volga Regional Archaeological Expedition started systematic excavations of this ruin.

For example, a large aristocratic house was excavated here. Two symmetrical entrances, at the midpoints of its northern and southern walls, led to a central hall. After passing through the entrance, a visitor would reach a hall with a brick-paved floor and narrow brick benches topped with wooden boards. A small pool occupied the center of the room. Further on, there is a massive platform, where the home's owner once had his seat. Alongside this platform were two exits, through which one could reach the northern aivan or leave the house (Figure 24). It is easy to picture this hall during official ceremonies and receptions, when the head of the household sat on the elevated platform under a canopy, while guests and relatives stood around the pool or sat along the walls at a respectful distance.

Figure 22. Carved alabaster column, Selitrennoe. Height 13.6 cm. (State Historic Museum, Moscow)

Two large and completely empty rooms stood at the sides of the central hall. These, probably, were also formal halls. Ceremonies and receptions held a special significance in the life of this house's inhabitants. Only three rooms had couches and heating (Plate 4). There was also a small courtyard with columns along the walls, and a storage room. Wooden houses for servants were built near the large house.

This is how the house looked in the middle of the 14th century, but during the next twenty to thirty years it was rebuilt several times. Some of the rooms were repeatedly partitioned in half, with the new dividing walls running in different directions each time. The entrances to other rooms from the central hall were blocked off, so that they became accessible only from the courtyard, while the entrances to other rooms from the courtyard were blocked and accessible only from the central hall. Old doors were closed off and new ones made in the walls. There was an attempt to expand the living area: a large family unit was broken up into smaller ones, formal halls were refurbished to be used as living rooms, and suites and individual rooms were completely separated from one another—it is clear that members of the household did not get on well with each other and tried to separate their living areas.

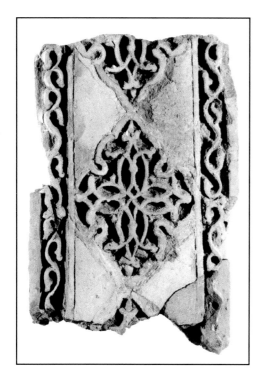

Figure 23. Fragment of a carved terra-cotta tile. Width 12 cm. (Astrakhan

A similar picture of an unstable society, anxiety, and the dissolution of large families leading to repeated remodeling was revealed by the excavation of another large, even richer house on the Selitrennoe site. This was a multiroomed palace with a huge central hall. The floor was paved with hexagonal tiles and rectangular bricks, creating an effect similar to patterned parquet. The center of the hall was occupied by a large washstand with a drainage well in the floor. A square elevation at the far end of the hall was paved with bricks, apparently for the seat of the head of the household—an eminent dignitary or aristocrat (Plate 5).

To the right and to the left of the central hall were rooms for living and housekeeping, with benches, stoves, and wash-stands (Plates 6–8). These floors, as well as the floors in the corridors, were paved with brick. A flat clay disk with a groove around it—the support for a millstone—was found in one of the rooms; apparently, this was a home mill. Another room, evidently a bakery, had stoves for baking flat bread. This palace also had a bath with a pool, lined with brick, and a plumbing system of clay pipes and gutters.

The walls of the central hall were whitewashed and decorated with lustre-glazed tiles (Plates 69–71, 79, Catalogue Nos. 40–42, 52). Some other rooms had paintings on the white plaster. A square board for some kind of game was scratched on the plaster covering a bench in a room which had perhaps served as a nursery. This room's walls were covered with graffiti drawn by children and adults: animals, the more terrifying the better, a person wearing a crown (Figure 25), and so on. There were also inscriptions in Arabic and the Uighur script. Adjoining the house was a large bath complex, with rooms warmed by heating flues under the floor, and rooms cooled in the summer with large pools.

This house was apparently first built in the 1330s, but it was soon rebuilt. From the 1370s to the 1390s it ceased being a palace and served as a dwelling for some commoners, possibly potters. The brick paving in both rooms and corridors became dilapidated, but

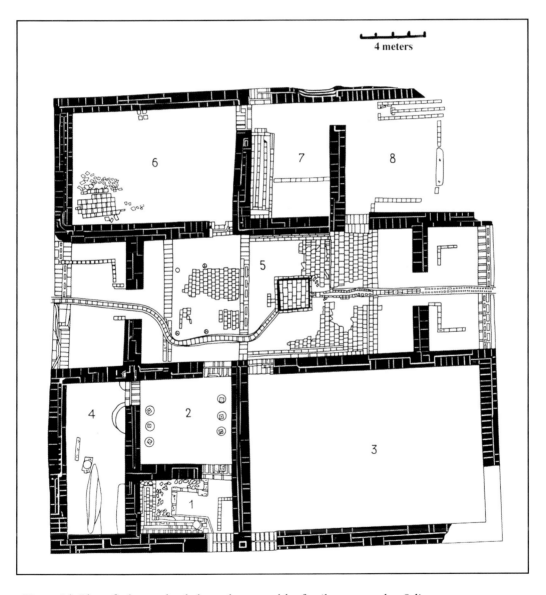

Figure 24. Plan of a house that belonged to a wealthy family, excavated at Selitrennoe.

Figure 25. Drawing on plaster of a house that belonged to a wealthy family, excavated at Selitrennoe. Maximum dimension 11 cm. (State Historic Museum, Moscow)

no attempt was made to restore it, and in some corridors the brick was replaced by earthen floors. Many rooms were rebuilt and divided into smaller sections. The walls of the swimming pool were dismantled and the bath was turned into an ordinary room.

The aristocratic palatial homes excavated on the Selitrennoe site suffered the same fate at about the same time, in the 1360s and 1370s. This was the period of internecine wars in the Golden Horde, when different groups of the aristocracy fought amongst themselves to gain power, and each new khan on his accession to the throne prosecuted his unsuccessful opponents. Archaeology lets us trace the process of how severely the city patricians who took part in these struggles suffered for it: drawn into these bloody seditions, their partisans energetically annihilated one another. Excavations at Tsarev revealed a similar picture. For example, a rich manor excavated there had been destroyed in the 1360s. The khan who had seized power in the capital at the time ordered a fortification line to be built which crossed this manor, and so completely eliminated it.

In addition to the private bath in the aristocratic palace home at Selitrennoe, a public bath was also excavated, which served the needs of the well-to-do members of the city's population. An entrance led to this bath from a square containing a mosque. A visitor would come first into an unheated hall, with patterned brick pavement on the floor, a fountain in the center, and windows with glazed alabaster grills (Plate 82, Catalogue No. 55). The bath had a drainage channel for waste water, with a settling tank. There were also two heated dressing rooms, warmed by a heating system under the floor, and laid out in the cross-shaped pattern typical of oriental public baths.

Chapter 12

The Craft Shops

During excavations on the Tsarev site, a shop was found where kashi tiles had been produced. Conceivably, the owner of this shop had his own household as a representative of the semi-free poor segment of the population. Before starting his work, this craftsman had to prepare the material from which the kashi tiles were made. As the material was usually in short supply, the craftsman probably arranged with builders who used his product to bring unusable waste fragments to him. He would crush them with stones and then grind them with millstones to a fine powder, which he would then mix with specially prepared clay. After this, he had to form the tiles themselves, and when they were dry, he covered one surface with a glaze made from special glass-forming components, like siliceous sand, with a coloring oxide added to it. He mixed this glazing material thoroughly with water and spread the creamy mixture over the surface of the tile, which was then left to dry. When fired, the kashi turned white and colored glazes reflect beautifully.

Finally, the crucial moment of firing the tile came, when it was easy to completely ruin all the work that had gone into making it. The slightest overheating of the kiln would spoil the whole job. If the tiles were positioned the wrong way, they would stick together. Great skill was needed to distribute the prepared tiles along the special shelves inside the kiln, set on rods extending from the walls of its firing chamber, and to lay them out with clay paddings to strengthen them, so that the high temperatures would not cause them to buckle and ruin the design. Then the firing began. Using the simplest of techniques, such as opening and closing the draft, an aperture at the top of the kiln, adding fuel at just the right moment, and observing the color of the heat, the craftsman could attain the exact temperature required without a thermometer, or any knowledge of physics. He had to determine by experience how much fire was needed to prevent the clay from cracking, how much more to melt the glaze to the point when it formed a liquid mass with a certain degree of fluidity, and how to allow the dyes to blend correctly with the glass, without fading or turning brown.

The owner of this shop specialized in two types of product. He made bricks with one side covered in blue, white, and yellow glaze, which were used to decorate walls. He also manufactured large slabs covered with a layer of glaze on one side. From these slabs another craftsman, probably at the construction site, would cut pieces of mosaic, which were then assembled and applied to the walls of palaces and mosques. Although our craftsman produced materials for work on large-scale construction jobs, this did not prevent him from making some earnings on the side by fashioning small toys: birds, horses, and rams, constructed from the clay in the workshop and covered with leftover glaze; they may even have been fired together with the tiles. The entire northern part of the city was inhabited by such craftsmen and retailers, people with common urban vocations (Figure 20, Plan).

At Selitrennoe, another potter's workshop turned out to be completely different. This large shop, with more than forty kilns, produced nearly every type of tableware as well as architectural elements (Plates 67–81, 83–105, Catalogue Nos. 37–54, 56–98). The materials found here allow us to determine the sequence of major operations in the potter's work, and provide an invaluable basis for studying the varied equipment and accessories used in the firing process, as well materials that comprised the clays and glazes. Many other kilns were studied in other areas of Selitrennoe, and at Tsarev and Vodiansk. Hundreds of bowls and thousands of fragments produced in these shops are now in museums (Figure 26, Plates 83–105, Catalogue Nos. 56–98).

We can now form a picture of how this craft was organized. There were highly specialized, privately owned shops that produced a small volume of a limited assortment of goods. The owner of such a shop took the risk of working on his own and paying city taxes or a quitrent to his master. The shop at Tsarev was one of these: apart from his side business of making toys, its owner produced only colored glazed bricks and slabs for mosaics. A kiln from another such privately owned shop was excavated at Vodiansk; this potter produced only certain types of unglazed ware.

Then there were estate shops, where dependent craftsmen of various professions worked for the owner of an estate. These shops, too, were highly specialized. For example, a potter who worked in an estate excavated on the Tsarev site produced only two types of ware, using two identical kilns. On another, rather small estate, lived a goldsmith, whose tiny shop was adjacent to the owner's home.

Some of the estate shops were much larger and produced a greater variety of materials, although these were rather the exception than the rule. Large shops with many kilns, technological division of labor, a varied assortment of products, and unified management constituted a special form of work organization. Here, several dozen craftsmen were united in one venture, owned by a rich or prominent person. As we have already seen, this type of craft shop, using forced labor and possibly slaves, was widely known in the Islamic Middle East and, as noted above, was called in Persian a *karkhanah* or work house. This era, in general, is characterized by the growth of slave labor in manufacturing, as karkhanahs were widespread throughout the Middle East: in Egypt, Iran, India, as well as Central Asia. Apparently they existed in the Golden Horde as well; the large pottery shop excavated at Selitrennoe was probably one.

Figure 26. White clay jug from the Tsarev. Height 24.9 cm. (State Hermitage, Saint Petersburg)

The excavated artifacts let us date this large shop to the 1370s and 1380s. Before then, the site was occupied by an estate, on which there were also several potters, and which was destroyed in the 1360s. When the estate was demolished, its walls were destroyed and a large assemblage of kilns appeared in its place, lying directly on the remains of the walls and even beyond its borders. What happened? Did the estate's craftsmen rebel, destroy their oppresor's house, and organize a free commune of craftsmen? Certainly not. Such a utopia would never occur in that epoch—even Campanella, the author of the City of the Sun, had not been born yet, and even in later times uprisings of this sort would end in tragedy. A more likely interpretation of the archaeological data is that the estate vanished during the internecine wars between the different groups of nobility, and its grounds became a karkhanah where some of the estate's former inhabitants—the potters—continued to work.

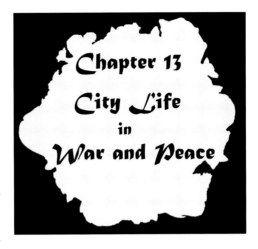

Chapter 13
City Life
in
War and Peace

A person creates around himself his own environment, filled with objects that reflect his personality and are part of his life. Would a description of this material environment help us to understand him? Would a reconstruction of ancient daily life let us, in the early 21th century, feel closer to those times long past—to the psychology, the world view, and the behaviour of our ancient predecessors, all those things about which we know so little? Understanding the living environment of past generations, and their values—what they thought of as wealth, and what the extent of poverty and lawlessness could be—is surely one of the most important parts of any exploration of the past. How did they work, what did they do in their free time, where did they live and how did they eat, what did they use to decorate their houses and to dress themselves? All this is very important for a historian.

During the period of the flourishing and political unity of the Golden Horde, the roads were safe and city dwellers had no need to fortify their cities. There was little unrest in the country. Physical anthropologists have shown that the skeletons of people buried in the urban cemeteries of the Golden Horde bear few traces of wounds or traumas received in battle. But the city dwellers did have weapons, including iron swords and sabers, daggers and spears, bows and arrows (including whistling arrows), maces, and distinctive battle-axes. They had plate armor and hauberks, and helmets which often had iron masks protecting the face. Bone and bronze rings with ridges were used to protect the thumb of the right hand from the bowstring when shooting (the so-called Mongolian technique). The Golden Horde's army was equipped with primitive artillery, such as different kinds of stone-throwing devices and arbalests, as well as catapults for casting rocks over walls, and vessels filled with a burning petroleum mixture, the so-called Greek fire. The people of the Golden Horde sometimes fought on camels.

Apparently, the types of armament used by the city dwellers and by the nomads were in most cases the same. Piano Carpini describes a spear with a hook for yanking horsemen from the saddle; such a spearhead was found on the Tsarev site. Detachments of city dwellers participated in the Golden Horde armies: there were regiments from Caffa, Krim, Azaq, and Bolgar among the troops of Mamay and Toqtamish.

A religious brotherhood of craftsmen, known as the *akhi*, spread from Asia Minor to the western parts of the Golden Horde, as far as Krim and Azaq, where Ibn Battuta met one of its members. Associated with the akhi were youth organizations whose members cultivated friendship, courage, military exercises and sports, and chivalry. At the same time, they enjoyed a rather free and easy lifestyle, sometimes rendering aid to the poor at the expense of violence against the rich. They were also responsible for various excesses, being implicated in incidents and scandals within the city.

The home environment of the middle and upper classes was well developed and very comfortable. Houses were lit with oil lamps of both ceramic and metal, as well as candles. Ceramic and metal candlesticks are also known from archaeological finds, and there is even one of marble, with rich decoration and inscriptions, which no doubt came from a wealthy household. Prosperous houses and public buildings were lighted by hanging glass lamps of Arabian craftsmanship, and by chandeliers holding several such lamps. Alabaster grills with plain or colored glass were set in windows (Plate 82, Catalogue No. 55). The rooms were full of pottery (rich houses had much expensive glazed dinnerware), as well as glass and sometimes even imported porcelain.

Braziers were widely used. Food was cooked in the living room—even the manors and homes of the wealthy had no separate kitchens. Ovens were well suited to baking flat bread. After pre-heating the oven, round pieces of dough were slapped onto its walls, and the flat bread was ready in a short time. Poor, middle-class, and even upper-class homes all had the same type of stove. During the summer, food may have been cooked outdoors over open fires.

The layout of common people's houses was standard: a nearly square room with a bench about a meter wide along three of its walls (Figure 27). The inhabitants of a house might discuss the city news and their own affairs while sitting on carpets and felts spread over these benches. At night, the same benches were spread with bedclothes, turning the room into a bedroom. Beneath the benches ran horizontal heating channels, which led from the stove to a vertical chimney standing in a corner. This heating technique was borrowed from the Chinese, who called this system of stoves with horizontal heating channels a kan. The hot kan kept the benches warm long after the fire in the stove went out (Plates 4–8).

No wooden furniture has survived and we know nothing of it, though some sources contain references to carved wooden benches. Judging from the small area of the floor space and how little of the walls was free from benches, there must have been practically no furniture against the walls. Reed mats covered the floors.

Floors were paved with baked bricks, which always remained dry and clean. Some rooms had a washbasin: a square brick or marble slab with a hole in the center was placed in the floor. Water ran though the hole to a large vessel with its base removed, or to a brick-lined space beneath the floor. The water was then absorbed into the ground while the floor itself remained dry.

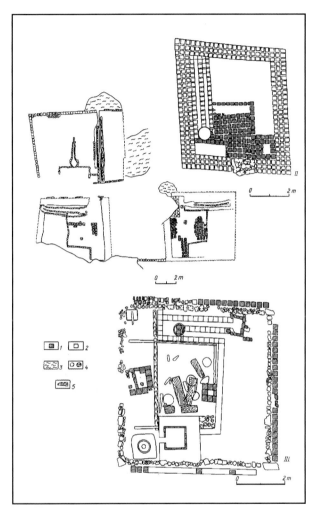

Figure 27. Houses of commoners excavated on the Vodiansk site: 1—baked bricks; 2—adobe bricks; 3—ash; 4—stones; 5—wood

Finds of bronze and iron door fittings, often covered with abundant ornamention and inscriptions, came from rich dwellings. Sometimes massive rings of cast bronze were hung upon the doors. There are many locks, both large and small, used to secure chests of different sizes (Plate 107, Catalogue Nos. 100, 101).

A rich household stands out mainly by the presence of expensive objects, especially imported ones. Even in the most well-to-do houses, the living rooms had no special conveniences, and were not especially large. Significant portions of rich houses were occupied by empty rooms intended for use in ceremonies, meetings, and receptions.

One important problem was the city's water supply. The poor sections had public wells and cisterns at street crossings. Rich houses had their own reservoirs, used solely for the needs of the estate. Along the narrow streets ran ditches, similar to the *aryks* of Central Asia and Iran, and beside these were laid sidewalks paved with brick fragments. Gutters made of hollowed-out tree trunks were laid in the ground to carry away waste water. As a rule, there were no conduits bringing water into the houses. One rich house at Selitrennoe, however, did have a channel to bring water to the large reception hall's central basin. Gutters and pipes for removing water from a room with a bath were found in another house at Selitrennoe, though this is a unique example. In most cases, bathing took place in separate bathhouses, both public and private, as we have seen— only very rich people had baths in their homes.

There were no basements. One large house at Selitrennoe had a storage room with pits for keeping foodstuffs. Cellars for wooden kegs are known, which were dug out at a distance from the houses. An effort was made to keep the courtyards adjacent to the houses clean and dry, for example by digging drainage ditches to prevent puddles and dampness around houses.

Yurts were sometimes set up in the courtyards, within the private grounds. Outside, in the narrow streets two carts could hardly pass each other. There were few, if any, wide streets that traversed the entire city. It was easy to lose one's way in the countless twists and turns and the infinite maze of small streets that came to dead ends, or brought one out into an open square, often with a large reservoir. Garbage and sewage were emptied directly into the street and the aryks. Stench, filth, and of course epidemics, were rampant in the city. It is not surprising that the dreaded plague, the "Black Death," managed to pass from Asia to Europe by way of the Golden Horde in the 14th century.

The people of the time played dice games and chess. There are findings of children's toys: tiny stone and ceramic vessels and figurines of animals. Children played at knucklebones, using talus bones (astragali) of rams, sometimes filled with lead. Another popular game consisted of taking turns, according to set rules, at placing counters on an intricate map of "Babylon" drawn on a slab, a brick, or even on the plaster covering a bench. Games of this type are known in the Caucasus and among Arab peoples, and were played by Russians until recent times.

Childhood is rather poorly and rarely represented in the records of medieval culture, but nonetheless it does reveal itself from time to time. Among the waste material around a kiln at Selitrennoe was a bowl that seems to have been made by a child, probably one of the potter's family. A man on a bird, drawn in a child's hand, is surrounded by a primitive pattern that was never finished (Plate 105, Catalogue No. 98). Small children were kept clean, as witness the frequent finds of hygienic devices used in cradles: ceramic and glass receptacles for waste.

The walls of rich houses were often covered with plaster, which was sometimes painted. The plaster was frequently used as a drawing and writing surface and renovated with new layers. People also wrote on bones; there is a find of an ox-bone, with a drawing of two mugs and an inscription in Polovtsian: "Caricature, swear to Allah! Ali . . . son of Muhammad put this here with his own hand." Turkic verses were scratched on a large jar from New Sarai: "Depriving me of my honor and glory, you took away my golden bowl. Filling the bowl with pure wine, [you] turned it to gold."

Sulfur and mercury were apparently used to combat skin diseases. Pieces of sulfur and sulfur in glass vessels are sometimes found in the cultural stratum of Golden Horde houses. The gardens of rich estates contained fountains, whose bronze pipes topped with lion heads have survived, and which were decorated with stone vases on pedestals.

Judging from the bone remains in the cultural strata of the Golden Horde sites (Tsarev, Selitrennoe, Vodiansk, Azov, and Majar), the majority of livestock consisted of ovicaprids (40–77%) and cattle (11–45%). Horse bones are fewer, and there are very small quantities of bones from camels, dogs, cats, gazelles, foxes, hares, aurochs, and various birds. The cattle of the Golden Horde were larger than those of the Russians. The almost complete absence of pig bones can be attributed to the influence of Islam. Oxen were used as draft animals, which explains why their bones are relatively numerous among the cattle. Horse harnesses included straps with bosses or conchae, bits, and stirrups. Saddles had high wooden pommels faced with leather, and iron cinch buckles. Horses were shod, and cattle were hung with large bronze bells when out to pasture.

About the city dwellers' eating habits we know very little. The vegetable and fruit components of their diet are known only from the remains discovered during excavations: grains of rye and wheat, walnuts, hazelnuts, acorns, almonds, raisins, plums, peaches, pistachios, cloves, pepper, beans, and coffee. The makeup of the meat diet is seen in the study of animal bones, and characteristic marks on the bones show that not only cattle were a source of meat, but horses and camels were eaten too. Game and fish were part of the diet, and egg shells of domesticated fowl are also present. Both nomads and city dwellers drank an intoxicating brew called *buza*, a kind of beer.

Ibn Battuta provides some information on cooking and the setting of the table. He relates that after a feast at Sarai, a four-legged vessel shaped like a "cradle" was set upon the table, covered with a mat of date leaves apparently brought from Egypt. This was filled with pastries, a roasted ram's head, four deep-fried flat cakes filled with sweets and covered with halva, and a tray of sweets; all were covered with a cotton cloth. Ibn Battuta also says that in Sarai he saw pies of puff pastry filled with chopped meat that had been boiled with almonds, walnuts, pistachios, onion, and other condiments. Bronze mortars and pestles containing currants, also used in food preparation, have been found on the Golden Horde sites (Figure 28).

Ibn Battuta also left us a description of a festival and feast to mark the end of the fast. On the morning of the day of the festival, the khan himself rode out on horseback amid his huge army of troops, accompanied by his entourage and consorts in wagons. His daughter rode with him, with a crown on her head, and his sons followed him with their regiments. Soothsayers and sheikhs, qadis, imams, and the sharif had departed earlier on horseback with the chief *qadi* at their head. Banners fluttered and kettledrums rumbled. The chief qadi delivered a sermon. The khan, along with his sons and heirs, his chief consort, and his kinsmen took seats in wooden tower-pavilions with benches for the emirs, or generals, and princes set up next to them.

Then a shooting competition began. After an hour, robes of honor were brought and each emir was invested with robe. As he put it on he would come to the foot of the khan's pavilion and make homage. Then a saddled and bridled horse was brought to this emir, which he led himself to his seat. This, apparently, was a ceremony of giving gifts from the khan to the emirs. Then the festive crowd of emirs paraded before the khan and his consorts, who remained seated in their richly decorated carriages, and entered a huge ger, its roof supported by four wooden columns covered with plaques of gold-plated silver and topped by capitals of silver gilt that gleamed and flashed. The floor of the tent was carpeted with silk rugs. Everyone took their seats around the khan's throne, which was of inlaid wood, its planks covered with a large rug. In the centre of this immense couch was a cushion, on which sat the khan and his chief consort. Next to them, their daughter and a consort sat on another cushion, and two other consorts on a third one. To the right of the couch a chair was placed, on which sat the heir to the throne, and to the left of it a chair on which the second son sat. Further to the right and left were places for the princes and emirs.

After this the feast began. The food, which was served on tables of gold and silver, consisted of boiled horsemeat and mutton. Meat cutters entered, wearing silken robes with silken aprons, and sheathed knives in their belts. Each table was served by its own meat cutter. A small platter of gold or silver was brought, containing salt dissolved in water, and gold and silver drinking vessels. The drink was mainly honeyed wine. The khan and consorts received wine from a daughter or son, while the heir apparent was served by emirs and princes. All this was followed by bowing and singing. Opposite the mosque another tent was erected for the clergy: qadis, khatibs, sharifs, and sheikhs, whose feast was arranged and served much the same as in the khan's tent. Wine skins

Figure 28. Bronze mortar (left) and pestle (right) from the Vodiansk site. Length of pestle 13.5 cm. (**Volgograd Museum of Local Lore**)

filled with kummis—fermented mare's milk—were distributed among the people. Afterward the Friday prayers were held in the mosque, and then the khan and his ensemble returned to their ger, where the feast continued until the evening prayer.

Both the city dwellers and the nomads of the Golden Horde used many foreign textiles: silks, brocades, cotton, as well as furs from the North. Although the nomads' dress was well described by 13th century travelers, that of the city dwellers is practically unknown from these sources, but we do now have some evidence from the archaeological data. A caftan sewn from patterned silk, with long narrow sleeves, was found in a rich woman's grave in a mausoleum in Ukek. This caftan reached to the knees, widening at the bottom, and was decorated with buttons and loops of plaited black silk cord. Another, larger caftan was worn over this first one; it had wide sleeves and reached the heels, and was decorated with silver embroidered patterns and ribbon trim. Braided decorations and what may be buttons made of cord were found at Tsarev and Selitrennoe. Another silk caftan from Ukek was tailored and fitted tight to the body; this one had a short skirt and no sleeves, and buttoned up to its low collar.

To judge from the archaeological materials, some types of clothing were common to both nomads and city dwellers, for example the *bokka*. The Simferopol treasure contains one silver ornament for a headdress that was apparently a kind of bokka, like that found in the Ukek mausoleum: a cap of red silk with winglike projections on the sides. It was fastened at the back with ribbons tied in bows and above it rose a hollow cylinder, covered with silken fabric and silver plaques. To the top of this cylinder was attached a gilded wooden board, also covered with silk and ornaments of silver wire. There are finds of both footwear and clothing made of leather, and small high boots made of silk and tied with silk laces were also found in the mausoleum at Ukek.

We also have a description of the appearance and apparel of Khan Batu:

A scanty beard, a large yellow face; his hair combed behind the ears; in one ear is a golden ring with a precious stone; a silk caftan is upon him; a pointed cap is on his head and golden belt with precious stones on the green Bolgar leather [is on his waist]; boots of red shagreen are on both legs. He has no sword at his waist, but there are black twisted horns covered with gold in his girdle.'

There is information that Khan Janibeg ordered everyone to wear turbans and broad straight gowns. Ibn Battuta wrote that sheepskin overcoats and caps were common in Majar, and that women wore small caps decorated with peacock feathers.

Both wooden combs and mirrors were widely used. As among many other peoples, mirrors had some magical properties, they were an integral part of female life and are found only in female burials. There are bronze tweezers, apparently articles of toiletry, small glass vessels, and a great number of various pieces of jewelry: earrings, bracelets, plaques, and so on (Figure 29, Plates 108, 109, Catalogue Nos. 108–112, 114–116). A rich house at Selitrennoe produced wooden spokes, probably from a stylish umbrella, which served as a symbol of power and prominence among many peoples of the East, including the Mongols.

Figuare 29. Bronze bracelet , Selitrennoe site. Length 4.3 cm. (Astrakhan Historic Architectural Museum)

Chapter 14
Religious Matters

In the 13th century the Golden Horde became an arena of religious struggle. Originally, the khans were shamanists. It was Khan Berke who adopted Islam from Central Asian shaikhs and began spreading it among his ulus. A mosque was built in Bolgar during his time. Later, the pagan khans came to power again. There were also khans who were Christians. In the end, Islam won the final victory in the 14th century, under Khan Özbeg.

A large mosque was excavated at the Vodiansk (Figure 30, left). The surviving stone foundations show that its rectangular hall was divided by rows of columns into six naves. The mihrab, a niche pointing in the direction of the holy city of Mecca, was set in the southern wall. An alabaster slab with a quotation from the Qur'an was mounted on the wall above it, and beyond it was a pavilion with wooden columns.

Inside this structure a large piece of a Classical marble column was dug into the ground, apparently to serve as a support for the Qur'an. When we discovered this column we were dumbfounded—where did this column come from, and how did it get to a Golden Horde city? With great effort we managed to get it out of the ground, and yet another surprise was waiting for us—beneath the column there was a fragment of a Corinthian marble capital! The Mongols must have transported these marble architectural elements an enormous distance—probably from some ancient city they had looted in the Crimea, possibly Chersonesus—to reuse them not in their original function, but as an interior support. Such were the times, as yesterday's nomads became the builders of today's cities.

Adjoining the corner of this mosque was the square socle of a minaret. The minaret itself, however, was round in plan. In the rubble we found arch-shaped bricks, some of them with turquoise glaze, and alabaster tablets bearing inscriptions in Arabic.

Another large prayer mosque was excavated at Selitrennoe. Beyond its richly decorated entrance lay an interior courtyard with a round cistern. The rest of the area was filled with wooden columns on brick bases. The central passage between the columns, leading to the mihrab, was wider than the others. Two columns in front of the mihrab were probably made of stone. There were two additional small entrances in the middle of the side walls. Some kind of ancillary structure, lavishly decorated with lustre glazed tiles (Plate 72, Catalogue No. 43), was built outside near the main entrance.

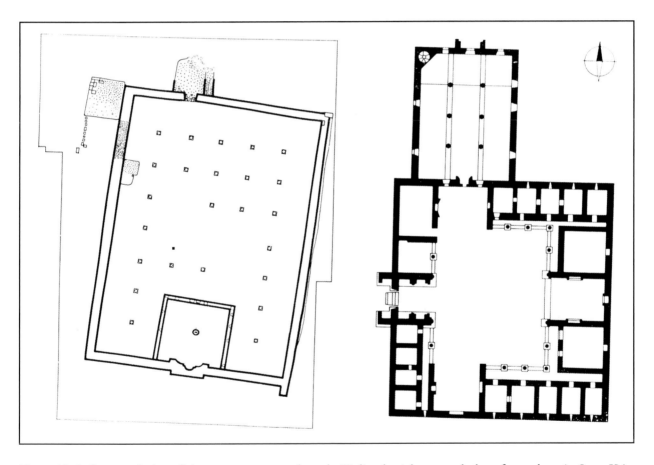

Figure 30. Left–ground plan of the mosque excavated on the Vodiansk; right–ground plan of a madrasa in Stary Krim (Krim-Solkhat).

The monumental architecture of the Golden Horde cities developed along the same lines as the Muslim architecture of other countries. A madrasa, an Islamic religious school, survived in Stary Krim. Its layout was typical of a Muslim madrasa: large recesses connected by arched passageways surrounded the rectangular courtyard; beyond were rooms for students and teachers (Figure 30, right). In one corner of the madrasa lay a small mausoleum containing a tombstone decorated with glazed tiles. There was a fountain in the courtyard, and above the entrance carved stone ornamentation that resembled those found in contemporary buildings at Azerbaijan and in Asia Minor.

However predominant Islam may have been, relics of paganism survived throughout the Golden Horde. Though Islam strictly prohibits it, jewelry, adornments, and other objects were placed in graves, and in burying the dead they did not always turn the deceased's face towards Mecca, as Islamic burial practices require. City dwellers of the Golden Horde believed in the salutary and protective powers of amulets, a widespread notion throughout the Islamic East. Amulets could take the form of inscriptions on a piece of paper, slipped under the stone in a finger ring or placed in a box. This might be a simple bronze box, or a splendid golden one like that found in the Simferopol treasure (Plates 62, 63, CatalogueNos. 31–33). Sometimes a miniature Qur'an, or citations from the Holy Book, were placed in such boxes.

Bronze or golden tablets bearing religious inscriptions constituted another type of amulet (Plate 106, Catalogue No. 99). One such was found at Tsarev: a bronze plaque with a loop for suspension was covered on both sides with unreadable signs imitating Arabic letters, and four lines of a magical inscription in Arabic: "Prophetic contemplation of a star." Seven signs repeated on both sides of this amulet apparently represented the Arabic magical symbols, the so-called *seba khuatim*, which corresponded to seven Arabic letters in seven verses in a *sura* of the Qur'an, and to seven of the ninety-nine qualities of God, as well as to the seven angels, seven demons, seven days of the week, and seven planets. Also on this amulet is a grid containing obscure signs—a variant of the "magic square," which had lost its mathematical significance (Figure 31). Real magic squares contain numbers which when added up in any direction gave the same number. Such squares of nine units, inscribed in India ink, were also found on pottery shards and vessels on sites of the Golden Horde period. They also had protective powers and are known in many different cultures of the world. Several such shards were found in a bath at Selitrennoe—perhaps the protection of such an amulet was particulary necessary for a man when naked, unprotected by any clothing. Primitive human figurines cut from bronze or iron sheet have emerged during the excavation of the various cities, and were also placed in nomadic graves in the steppe. Among various tribes and peoples of Siberia, such figurines were thought to be repositories of a person's soul and spirit.

Figure 31. Bronze astral amulet from the Tsarev. Height 5 cm. (Museum of the Department of Archaeology, Kazan University)

Notwithstanding Islam's supremacy among the Golden Horde, missionaries from western Europe were busy there. They came to Sarai by way of Krim and Azaq, where there were Italian colonies. In the 13th century, western kings and popes sent envoys to the great khan in distant Mongolia, to try to persuade him to convert to Catholicism and ally himself with them, or even become a vassal of the papal throne. Even in the 14th century these hopes did not die. But in the Golden Horde, Catholicism met with strong opposition from the Russian orthodox clergy, whom the khans had allowed into their lands, permitting the practice of Orthodox Christianity, and even the founding of an Orthodox Metropolis in Sarai.

Thus shamanism, Islam, Catholicism, Orthodox Christianity, and even Buddhism crossed paths in the Golden Horde, clearly demonstrating this huge steppe empire's role as an intermediary between East and West. The historical importance of Russian colonies in the Golden Horde lay in the fact that they prevented Western Christianity from gaining a foothold in the Volga region, and to a certain extent paved the way for Orthodoxy to enter Russian society in the 16th century.

But this transition was inevitable. Already in the 15th century, dissension among the various Golden Horde states had become an obstacle to social development. The splendid flowers of the Golden Horde cities that blossomed here in the 14th century turned out to be barren, and the steppe overwhelmed them. The nomadic khanates that were the legacy of the Golden Horde lay as a stumbling block along the trade routes, and became a source of alarm and danger for their neighbors, and of hard times for their own people.

Chapter 15
The Diaster of 1395

$\mathcal{I}n$ the second half of the 14th century Timur, or Tamerlane as he was also known, created his mighty empire in Central Asia, and found a major rival in the Golden Horde. It was necessary for him to reduce the latter's importance by neutralizing the role of trading centers in the Volga area and in the Crimea, and breaking the threads of those trade routes that crossed its territory to connect East and West. Then, thought Tamerlane, caravans would have to go through Central Asia and Iran, thereby enabling him to establish a world empire under his own sword. Intending to begin by undermining the Golden Horde's power from within, he placed his ward, Khan Toqtamish, on the throne at Sarai, in the hope that he would become his obedient vassal.

Toqtamish, however, disappointed him as the khan turned out to be a major political figure. Idealizing the imperial Golden Horde in the time of Özbeg and Janibeg, when it had been united and strong and its mighty hand held a firm grip over the conquered peoples, he looked back to the days when the cities on the Volga had flourished, and the central power was not challenged by internecine wars and unruly princes.

In 1380, the Golden Horde suffered a terrible blow when Russian troops, under the command of prince Dmitri Ivanovich of Moscow, defeated the army of Mamay on the field of Kulikov. This was the beginning of the end of the Golden Horde. Toqtamish, who came to power the following year, determined to restore the former glory of his ancestors' state, first by regaining the obedience of Moscow. The successful campaign against Moscow ensured Russian compliance, but the subjugated peoples now knew that the Golden Horde was no longer invincible.

The second blow to the Golden Horde was dealt by Tamerlane. His troops met Golden Horde armies several times, but could not achieve final victory. From time to time Toqtamish reconciled with Tamerlane, but then once more they would return to their hostilities. Periodically, emirs who were in favor of a union with Central Asia gained the upper hand at Toqtamish's court, but then those with aggressive and unrealistic attitudes came back into power. In 1394, Tamerlane decided to finish the Golden Horde off. His troops passed through the gorges of Dagestan and entered the north Caucasian steppe from the south. Here, on the river Terek, the decisive battle between Tamerlane and Toqtamish's armies took place in 1395. When part of the Golden Horde troops betrayed Toqtamish, the die was cast, and Tamerlane won the decisive victory. Toqtamish's strength was broken, and the Central Asian conqueror burst onto the steppe of Eastern Europe. The cities of the Crimea and the Volga now lay in his path.

Nearly every excavated trench on the Tsarev —the ruins of New Sarai—shows signs of the city's destruction at the hands of Tamerlane's forces. Beneath the brick wreckage near the kiln in the tile shop lies the skeleton of a man, not buried. The remains of a child near one of the houses were also unburied; its lifeless body was left in an unnatural pose in the ruins of the house. People's unburied remains are often found in the poses they took in death during the slaughter, looting, and other atrocities committed by Tamerlane's warriors in the ruined and burning city. We found the skeletons of children who had tried to escape by hiding themselves in stoves and chimneys, and met their deaths there. Lying on the staircase leading to one of the excavated cellars was the skeleton of a man who had sought refuge in his own cellar, and was killed by a mortal blow from a dagger. The remains of people were hurriedly buried under the rubble of houses that stretched along walls. A similar picture is seen in the excavation of the Vodiansk site. Piles of skulls were found—it is possible that these were areas where the heads of the dead were collected for counting (Figure 32).

The year 1395 recalled the atrocities that the Mongols themselves had committed in the cities they captured 150 years before. Now those who lived in the cities of the Golden Horde shared the fate of the inhabitants of Samarkand and Merv, Riazan, and

Kiev, cities that the Mongols had destroyed in the 13th century. All were killed, save the beautiful women who could be sent to harems, and the strong and skilled craftsmen who could serve a useful purpose.

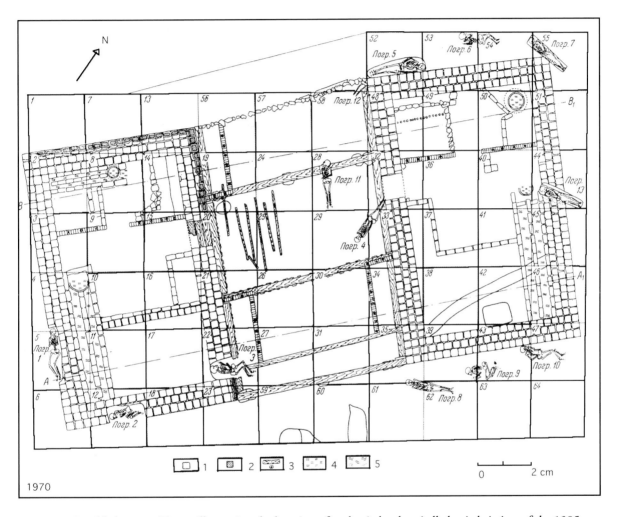

Figure 32. Double house at Tsarve illustrating the location of unburied or hurriedly buried victims of the 1395 catastrophe: 1—adobe bricks; 2—baked bricks; 3—wood; 4—ash; 5—charcoal

New Sarai did not survive the year 1395. Not everyone was killed or captured, but soon after the bloodbaths, life on the site died. The old capital, Sarai, managed to survive a little longer. Here, archaeologists did not find the same gruesome scenes as in the devastation of 1395. The city survived the catastrophe, those who were killed were properly buried in the cemeteries, and the survivors erased other traces of the destruction.

In the 15th century, however, this city too fell into decline, and vanished. Once more the silent steppe reclaimed the land where the will of the khans and the labor of craftsmen and builders had erected once flourishing cities. The cities of the Golden Horde were not an organic extension of the economic development of the lower Volga region. In this they were unlike the cities of Russia, Central Asia, and western Europe. Those cities had a history which the Golden Horde lacked; they appeared as the result of a long process of development as centers of trade and crafts, and had ties to their surroundings which gave them historical stability. In the Golden Horde, urban life appeared as the result of a policy ordered by the authorities, and was artificially supported by the power of the state. While the power of the khans was strong, and could ensure safety on the roads, and a constant influx of material and human resources to these cities, they flourished. But as soon as the central power weakened, the cities began to wither. One great military defeat was all it took to kill them, and soon only the memory of them remained.

After Tamerlane's destruction of the Golden Horde cities in the Volga, the trade routes shifted. Spices, silk, and other goods began to be sent to the Mediterranean by other routes through the Middle and Near East. Barbaro, an Italian traveler of the 15th century, wrote that ". . . before it [the city of Hajji-tarkhan, or Astrakhan] was destroyed by Tamerlane, all the spices and silk went to Tana through it. Now they go to Syria. Six or seven large galleys were sent annually to Tana to pick up these spices and silks from Venice alone. Neither Venetians nor representatives of other foreign nations conducted trade in Syria in these times."

It is very revealing that all the verbs were written in the past tense.

Chapter 16.

Conclusion

Much has been written about the differences, and even the oppositeness, of West and East. The people of the West, and above all Western Europeans, are supposed to have created modern science and made the historic breakthrough into modern history. But there were times when the Orient, and especially China, held the lead in the area of technical progress. China and India, it is said, have a "closed" outline, whereas Europe is broken up by numerous gulfs and seas—this factor, supposedly, promoted European trade and seafaring, and contributed to its diversity of languages and peoples. But there are numerous islands, convenient bays, and straits in the East as well. Some writers say that the small city-states of Greece developed a kind of "freedom of the spirit"—the democracy which later became the West's favored child. But the free spirit of city dwellers lived also in the East, and there too was found spiritual freedom and teachings that supported the inner independence of philosophers from the outside world. The power of logic and the consistency of critical and rational thought developed in the West, but they have not always held sway there, and they can easily be discerned in the teachings of the East as well. And as to individuality and personality—was this not completely oppressed in the Middle Ages and not resurrected until the Renaissance? Did it not redevelop in the shape of individualism in modern times, only to succumb to cruel and uncivilized totalitarian regimes in the same Europe? There is, to be sure, a peculiar dynamism in some periods of Western history, but so it is also in the East. Nor is the market economy a Western prerogative: it too existed in the Orient, even in the Middle Ages. Cities with their bazaars, trade caravans, and monetary economy all were well known in the countries of the East when the West was still struggling in the grip of a natural economy.

In contrast, we cannot deny that the East had never enjoyed a Renaissance, although it had existed in an embryonic form. There was nothing in the East comparable to the European Reformation of the 16th century, the century of the formation of modern man. This was the creation of a New Age that eventually overtook the world. Thus, there was something in the West which the East did not have and that, and this lack slowed down the broad cultural development in the East. These underlying questions will have to be addressed by the future research by historians and philosophers.

The mystery of history moves across centuries. As in the past, the West could not exist without the East. Though now and then estranged, and intently watching and measuring each another—all the while they are borrowing elements of each others' cultures and reworking them after into their own fashion, as the dialogue between two worlds goes on. Let us continue to believe in the unity of human history and the possibility of human solidarity.

The Plates

Plate 1. Burials of the Bronze Age and Sarmatian Period in a barrow near Krivaia Luka.

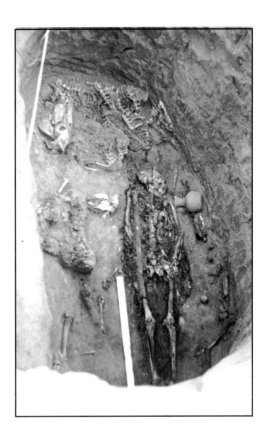

Plate 2. Burial of a warrior of the Khazar period in a barrow near Krivaia Luka, 10th century [top right]. Detail of burial [bottom].

Plate 3. Medieval mausoleum discovered under a mound near Krivaia
Luka (15th century).

Plate 4. A large house excavated at Selitrennoe. Side room.

Plate 5. A large house excavated at Selitrennoe. Two views [above and right].

Plate 6. A large house excavated at Selitrennoe. Central hall.

Plate 7. A large house excavated at Selitrennoe. Side room.

Plate 8. Overview of a large house excavated at Selitrennoe.

Plate 9. Aerial view of a large house excavated at Selitrennoe and bath house [center].

Plate 10. Bath house in a large house excavated at Selitrennoe. Overhead view.

Plate 11. Bath house excavated at Selitrennoe. Pillars supported the floor of the room that had a hypocaust heating system.

Plate 12. Crypt in the 14th century city cemetery excavated at Selitrennoe.

Plate 13. Buckle decorated with the depiction of sphinxes. Bronze with silver appliqué, burial near Baranovka. Catalogue No. 1.

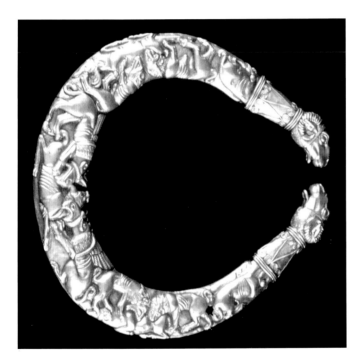

Plate 14. Torque. Gold, burial near Kosika. Catalogue No. 2.

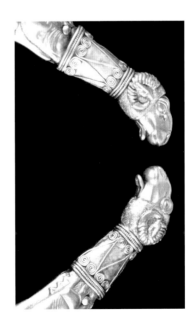

Plate 15. Torque. Gold, burial near Kosika. Catalogue No. 2.

Plate 16. Torque. Gold, burial near Kosika. Catalogue No. 2.

Plate 17. Bracelet. Gold, burial near Kosika [above]. Catalogue No. 3.

Plate 18. Bracelet. Gold, burial near Kosika. Detail: representation of carcasses of skinned sheep placed on the pelts [right]. Catalogue No. 3.

Plate 20. Bowl. Silver, burial near Kosika. Catalogue No. 5.

Plate 19. Plaque depicting an old man. Silver, burial near Kosika. Catalogue No. 4.

Plate 21. Tumbler, cylindrical. Silver, burial near Kosika. Catalogue No. 6.

113

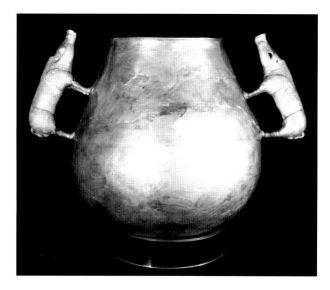

Plate 22. Vessel, called a *kubok*, with handles shaped in the form of wild boars. Silver, burial near Kosika. Catalogue No. 7.

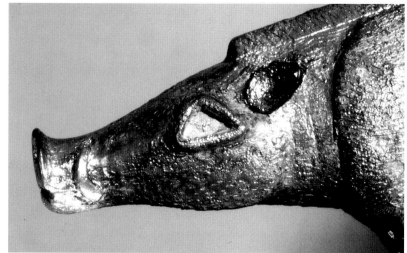

Plate 23. Detail of Plate 22. Handle, boar's head. Silver. Catalogue No. 7.

Plate 24. Detail of Plate 22. Handle in the form of a boar. Silver. Catalogue No. 7.

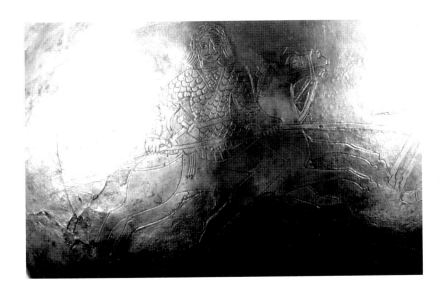

Plate 25. Detail of scenes on the body of vessel in Plate 22. Catalogue No. 7.

Plate 26. Detail of scenes on the body of vessel in Plate 22. Catalogue 7.

Plate 27. Phalerae from a horse bridle. Gold, burial near Kosika. Catalogue No. 8.

Plate 28. Detail of Plate 27. Catalogue No. 8.

Plate 29. Belt buckle in the form of a hedgehog. Gold with colored glass and stones, burial near Kosika. Catalogue No. 9.

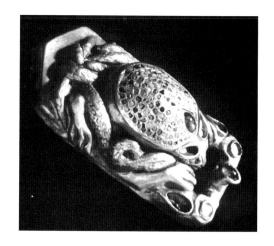

Plate 30. Side view of a belt buckle in Plate 29. Burial near Kosika. Catalogue No. 9.

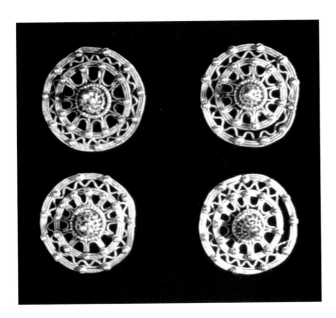

Plate 31. Ornaments wih boss in center. Gold, burial near Kosika. Catalogue No. 10.

Plate 32. Finial on a large whetstone. Gold, burial near Kosika. Catalogue No. 11.

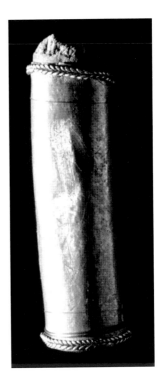

Plate 33. Finial. Gold, burial near Kosika. Catalogue No. 12.

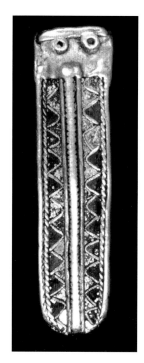

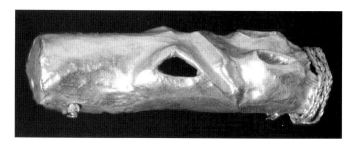

Plate 36. Finial in zoomorphic form. Gold, burial near Kosika. Catalogue No. 14.

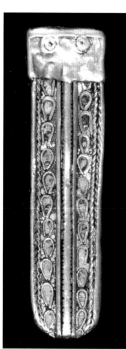

Plates 34-35. Belt terminals. Gold, burial near Kosika. Catalogue No. 13.

Plate 37. Effigy of a man. Turkish, stone-carved. Catalogue No 15.

Plate 38. Plate. Silver-gilt, burial in the Belorechen barrows. Catalogue No. 16.

Plate 39. Coins, part of a Golden Horde treasure. Gold, found near the village of Karatue in Tatarstan. Catalogue No. 17.

Plate 40–41 . Coin of the Sultans of Delhi (obverse, left; reverse, right). Gold, Simferopol treasure. Catalogue No. 18.

Plate 42. Coin of the Sultans of Delhi (obverse). Gold, Simferopol treasure. Catalogue No. 19.

Plate 43. Coin of the Sultans of Delhi (reverse). Gold, Simferopol treasure. Catalogue No. 19.

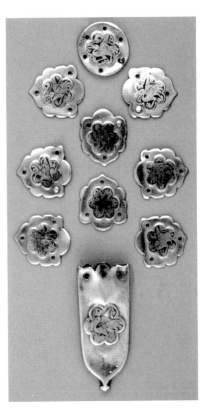

Plate 44. Belt ornaments. Gold, Simferopol treasure. Catalogue No. 20.

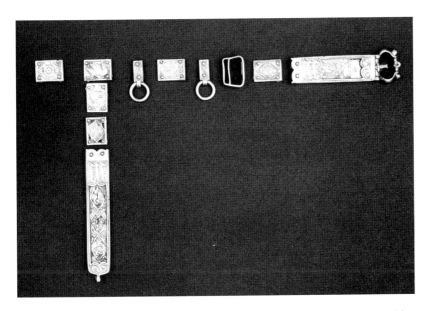

Plate 46. Belt ornaments. Silver, Simferopol treasure. Catalogue No. 21.

Plate 45. Detail of belt seen in Plate 44. Catalogue No. 20.

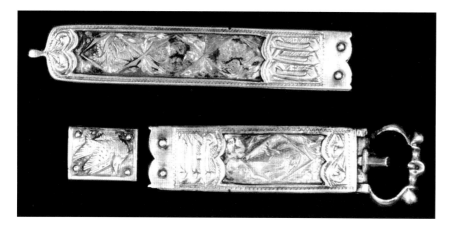

Plate 47. Cast-silver belt ornaments, Simferopol treasure. Catalogue No. 21.

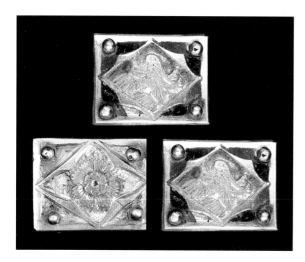

Plate 48. Belt plaques. Silver, Simferopol treasure. Catalogue No. 21.

Plate 49. Belt ornaments. Gold, inlaid with carnelian, Simferopol treasure. Catalogue 22.

Plate 50. Detail of belt ornaments in Plate 49, Simferopol treasure. Catalogue No. 22.

Plate 51. Bracelet with a Persian inscription. Gold, Simferopol treasure. Catalogue No. 23.

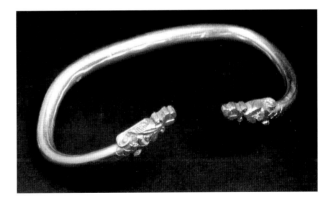

Plate 52. Bracelet with zoomorphic terminals. Gold, Simferopol treasure. Catalogue No. 24.

Plate 53. Chain for headdress. Inlaid with colored stones, set in gold, Simferopol treasure. Catalogue No. 25.

Plate 54. Plaques. Gold inlaid with colored stones, Simferopol treasure. Catalogue No. 26.

Plate 55. Plaque. Gold inlaid with turqouise and amethyst, Simferopol treasure. Catalogue No. 27.

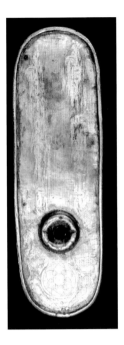

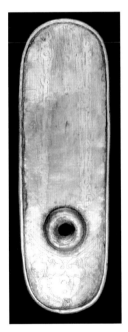

Plate 58-59. Divination cup. Silver, incised, Simferopol treasure. Exterior surface [above, right]; interior surface [right]. Catalogue No. 29.

Plates 56-57. P'ai-tzü, a symbol of authority. Silver, Simferopol treasure. Obverse [top, left]; reverse [bottom, left]. Catalogue No. 28.

Plate 60. Ladle with representations of an owl and a man on the handle finial. Silver, Simferopol treasure. Catalogue No. 30.

Plate 61. Details of finial illustrated in Plate 60, representations of an owl and a man, Simferopol treasure [top, right]. Catalogue No. 30.

Plate 62. Case for prayer texts illustrating the "knot of happiness," top center. Gold, Simferopol treasure. Catalogue No. 31.

Plate 63. Cases for prayer texts. Gold, Simferopol treasure. Catalogue Nos. 32, 33.

Plate 64. Belt ornaments in Chinese style. Silver-gilt, Simferolpol treasure. Catalogue No. 34.

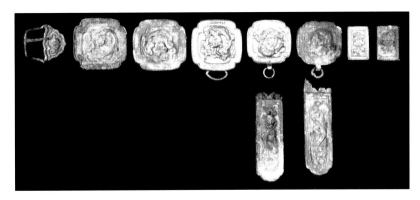

Plate 65. Fragments of a vessel. Glass with enamel painting, Selitrennoe. Catalogue No. 35.

Plate 66. Fragment of a vessel. Glass with enamel painting, Selitrennoe [right]. Catalogue No. 36.

Plate 68. Fragment a tile depicting a person. Painted lustreware, Selitrennoe. Catalogue No. 39.

Plate 67. Fragments of a mosaic. Ceramic, lustre glaze [above]; tile, glazed and painted [below], Selitrennoe. Catalogue No. 37, 38.

Plate 70. Tile sherds. Ceramic with painted lustreware [above], Selitrennoe. Catalogue No. 41.

Plate 69. Tile sherd. Ceramic with painted lustreware, Selitrennoe. Catalogue No. 40.

Plate 71. Tile sherds. Ceramic with painted lustreware, Selitrennoe. Catalogue No. 42

Plate 72. Tile fragment with lustreware painting, Selitrennoe townsite. Catalogue No. 43.

Plate 73. Tile fragments with lustreware painting, Selitrennoe townsite. Catalogue No. 44.

Plate 74. Tiles. Terracotta, carved and engraved, Selitrennoe. Catalogue Nos. 45, 46.

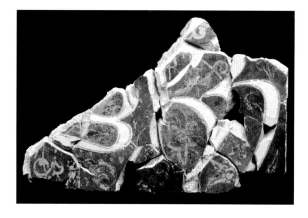

Plate 75. Tile sherd. Ceramic, painted, and glazed,
Selitrennoe. Catalogue 47.

Plate 76. Tile sherd. Ceramic,
painted, and glazed, Selitrennoe.
Catalogue No. 49.

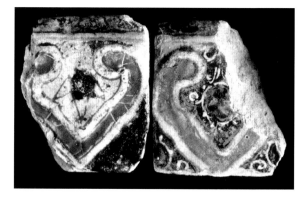

Plate 77. Tile border sherds. Ceramic, painted, and
glazed, Selitrennoe. Catalogue No. 50.

Plate 78. Tile with Persian inscription. Ceramic,
painted, and glazed, Selitrennoe. Catalogue No. 51.

Plate 79. Mosaic panel assembled from tiles. Ceramic, painted, and glazed, Selitrennoe townsite. Catalogue No. 52.

Plate 80. Mosaic medallion framed by a Persian inscription. Ceramic, painted, and glazed, Selitrennoe. Catalogue No. 53.

Plate 81. Architectural detail. Ceramic, glazed, Selitrennoe townsite. Catalogue No. 54.

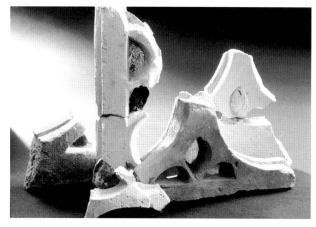

Plate 82. Fragments of a window grill. Alabaster, Selitrennoe townsite. Catalogue No. 55.

Plate 83. Bowl with the depiction of a centaur. Ceramic, painted, and glazed, Selitrenne. Catalogue 56.

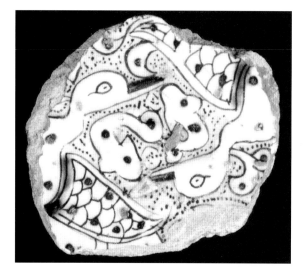

Plate 84. Fragment of a bowl with birds. Ceramic, painted, and glazed, Selitrennoe. Catalogue 57.

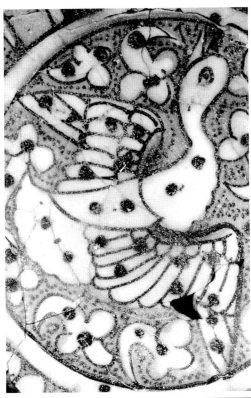

Plate 85. Fragment of a bowl with the depiction of a flying bird. Ceramic, painted, and glazed. Selitrennoe [left]. Catalogue No. No. 58.

Plate 86. Bowl. Glazed and painted, Selitrennoe [below]. Catalogue No. 59.

Plate 87. Two sherds from bowls [bottom and right] and an intact bowl [top left]. Ceramic, painted, and glazed, Selitrennoe. Catalogue Nos. 60-62.

Plate 88. Bowls. Ceramic, glazed, and painted, Selitrennoe. Catalogue Nos. 63, 64.

Plate 89. Bowls. Ceramic, painted, and glazed, Selitrennoe [above]. Catalogue Nos. 65-67.

Plate 90. Bowls. Ceramic, painted, and glazed, Selitrennoe [left]. Catalogue Nos. 68-70.

Plate 91. Bowls. Ceramic, painted, and glazed, Selitrennoe [bottom]. Catalogue 71, 72.

Plate 92. Bowls. Ceramic, painted, and glazed, Selitrennoe [above]. Catalogue Nos. 73, 74.

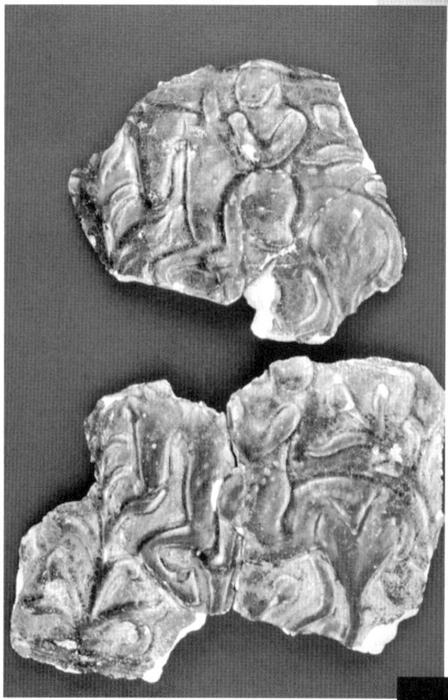

Plate 93. Fragments of a bowl depicting a polo game. Ceramic, incised and glazed, Selitrennoe. Catalogue Nos. 75.

Plate 94. Vase [left] and three misfired bowls [right]. Ceramic, glazed imitation celadon, Selitrennoe. Catalogue Nos. 76, 77.

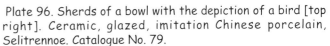

Plate 95. Sherds of a bowl with the depiction of a bird [left]. Ceramic, glazed, imitation Chinese porcelain, Selitrennoe. Catalogue No. 78.

Plate 96. Sherds of a bowl with the depiction of a bird [top right]. Ceramic, glazed, imitation Chinese porcelain, Selitrennoe. Catalogue No. 79.

Plate 97. Two sherds of a vessels [top and bottom] depicting birds. Ceramic, glazed, imitation Chinese porcelain. Sherd of a vessel with bird's head [center]. Ceramic, incised and glazed. Selitrennoe [left]. Catalogue Nos. 80–82.

Plate 98. Bowl. Ceramic, painted and glazed imitation Chinese porcelain, Selitrennoe [bottom]. Catalogue No. 83.

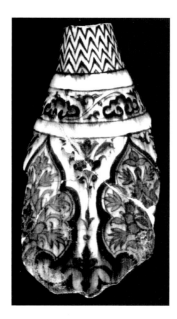

Plate 99. Sherd of a vessel. Ceramic, painted, and glazed imitation Chinese porcelain, Selitrennoe. Catalogue No. 84.

Plate 100. Two sherds of bowls. Ceramic, painted, and glazed imitation Chinese porcelain, Selitrennoe. Catalogue 85, 86.

Plate 101. Bowl with an inscription around the shoulder. Ceramic, painted, glazed lusterware, Selitrennoe. Catalogue 87.

102. Sherd of a bowl with a floral motif. Ceramic, incised and glazed, Selitrennoe. Catalogue No. 88.

Plate 103. Two bowls [left]. Ceramic, painted and glazed. Jug [right]. Terracota, unglazed. Selitrennoe. Catalogue Nos. 89-91.

Plate 104. Money boxes [left]. Terracotta, unglazed. Jugs [right]. Terracotta, nglazed. Selitrennoe. Catalogue Nos. 92 –97.

Plate 105. Bowl with a child-like drawing. Ceramic, painted, and glazed, but misfired, Selitrennoe. Catalogue No. 98.

Plate 106. Amulet with an Arabic inscription. Bronze, cast, Selitrennoe. Catalogue No. 99.

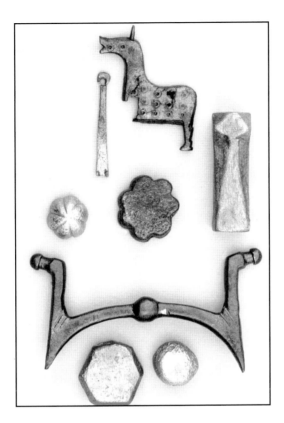

Plate 107. Articles of daily life and commerce, (key, lock in the shape of a horse, plaque, weights, anvil, and support), Selitrennoe. Catalogue Nos. 100–107.

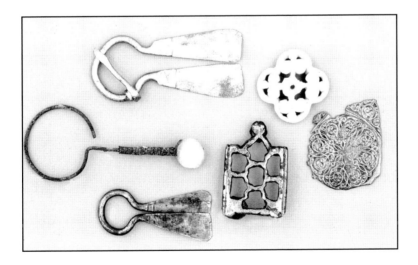

Plate 108. Clothing fasteners, ornaments, and jewelry, Selitrennoe. Catalogue Nos. 108–113.

Plate 109. Ornaments. Gold, Selitrennoe. Catalogue Nos. 114-116.

The Catalogue

Format of the Cataloguing

Field 1. The Cat. No. is the number assigned for cataloguing in this publication. This is followed the descriptive noun for the object; then the Plate number (illustration) for the object.

Field 2. The description of the object.

Field 3. The materials(s) from which the object is made, followed by the method(s) of construction.

Field 4. The dimension of the object.

Field 5. The date the object was manufactured.

Field 6. The loction where the object was found.

Field 7. The location where the object can be found today.

Field 8. The inventory or control number for the object at its present location.

The Catalogue

Cat. 1. Belt buckle (Plate 13)

Sarmatian belt buckle cast in bronze; lateral opening on one end and a hook for fastening into a loop on the opposite; prongs for securing. Female sphinx (torso); lion legs and paws; adorsed lion bodies with wings extending laterally; scene enclosed in frame. Pearls embelish the lion bodies.
Silver, bronze, pearls. Cast, stamped, inlaid.
Diameter: 7.6 cm. ; width: 4.6 cm.
1st century B.C.E.–1st century C.E.
Barrow 13, burial 1, burial ground near the village of Baranovka, Chernoiar region, Astrakhan oblast
Astrakhan Historic Architectural Museum
Inventory number KP 23453

Cat. 1

Cat. 2. Torque (neck ornament) (Plates 14, 15, 16)

Three scenes decorate the torque: in the center, two griffens attack a bull; at left, two lions attack a ram and a mythical creature with feline body and crested top; at right, a lion and lioness slaughter a deer. Finials in the form of rams' heads were taken from a torque of similar type and attached to this piece.
Gold. Cast, forged, soldered, stamped, riveted, chased.
Diameter (exterior): 17.5 cm.; (interior): 12.5 cm.
4th century B.C.E.
Burial 1, burial ground near Kosika village, Enotaev region, Astrakhan oblast
Astrakhan Historic Architectural Museum
Inventory number KP 35524

Cat. 2

Cat. 3. Bracelet, one side (Plates 17, 18)

Originally there were two parts that were were hinged, one side is now lost. Top register of the openwork reveals a row of stretched sheepskins afixed with nails; skinned carcasses laying on top. Second and third registers are geometric ornamentation with a running spiral around both egdes.
Gold. Cast, forged, soldered; wire drawn.
Width (top): 11.5 cm., (bottom):13.8 cm.; height: 13.0 cm.
4tth-3th centuries B.C.E.
Burial 1, burial ground near Kosika village, Enotaev region, Astrakhan oblast
Astrakhan Historic Architectural Museum
Inventory number KP 32527

Cat. 3

Cat. 4. Plaque (Plate 19)

Face of a bald man; long drooping mustache and pointed beard. The reverse side is concave, without a pin for attaching.
Silver. Cast.
Length: 2.2 cm.; width: 1.2 cm.
1st century C.E.
Burial 1, burial ground near Kosika village, Enotaev region, Astrakhan oblast
Astrakhan Historic Architectural Museum
Inventory number KP 35582

Cat. 5. Bowl (Plate 20)

1st century C.E.
Hemispherical body on a low base, flaring rim; two ring handles with attachment plates in the shape of vine leaves soldered onto body. The interior surface has depictions of four fish. Greek inscription near the rim: ". . . of the king Artawazd Ampasalak made. . . ." Place of production, Italy.
Gold, silver. Cast, soldered, chased, gilt.
Diameter at rim: 31.1 cm.; height: 15.3 cm.
1st century C.A.
Burial 1, burial ground near Kosika village, Enotaev region, Astrakhan oblast
Astrakhan Historic Architectural Museum
Inventory number KP 40898

Cat. 6. Tumbler or *situla* with lid (Plate 21)

Cylindrical body; slightly concave bottom; convex lid with rosette decoration. Incised on the sides in the upper register:: two bowman shooting at three flying birds. Lower register: fish, and birds resembling herons and ducks.
Gold, silver. Forged, soldered, engraved, gilt.
Diameter: 4.5 cm.; height: 6.7 cm.
1st century C.A.
Burial 1, burial ground near Kosika village, Enotaev region, Astrakhan oblast
Astrakhan Historic Architectural Museum
Inventory number KP 40891

Cat. 7. Vessel, *kubok* (Plates 22-26, fig. 5)

Globular-shaped body narrowing to rim; hollow handles in the form of wild boars, positioned vertically. The body is decorated with two friezes. Upper frieze: a boar being chased by dogs and mounted spearmen who are dressed in narrow trousers and short caftans. Lower frieze: battle scene that includes a heavily armed mounted warrior with spear, quiver, and sword; cavalrymen are dressed similar to those in the hunting scene above, and armed with bows and swords; a wounded horse has collapsed onto its front knees. Elements of the horse bridle and saddle are depicted in detail.
Gold, silver. Cast, riveted, engraved, gilt.
Diameter: 20.3 cm.; height: 21.1 cm.
1st century C.E.
Burial 1, burial ground near Kosika village, Enotaev region, Astrakhan oblast
Astrakhan Historic Architectural Museum
Inventory number KP 35560

Cat. 4

Cat. 5

Cat. 6

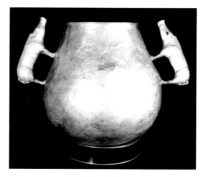

Cat. 7

Cat. 8. Phalerae from a horse's bridle. Two pieces (Plates 27, 28)

Identical convex discs, each with a large triangular setting for an inlay (now lost) in the center, surrounded by three griffen heads; a row of predators' heads around the traingle depicted so that the ear of each is in the open mouth of the next. Silver loops on the back for attaching with leather straps.
Gold, silver, colored glass or stones. Cast, riveted, stamped (?), chased, inlaid.
Diameter: 14.6; cm.; height: 2.4 cm.
1st century C.E.
Burial 1, burial ground near Kosika village, Enotaev region, Astrakhan oblast
Astrakhan Historic Architectural Museum
Inventory number KP 28747

Cat 8.

Cat. 9. Belt buckle. Two pieces (Plates 29 and 30)

Shaped like hedgehogs with small colored inlays on the backs. Two snakes stretch along the sides, their tails knotted together behind the hedgehogs. Griffen heads with large ears in front of the hedgehogs. At the back, each buckle has a soldered vertical plate, forming a small container with tiny hinged lids; also an aperture for attaching to a belt and a hook for fastening.
Gold, colored stones and glass. Forged, soldered, stamped, chased, inlaid.
Length: 7.0-7.1 cm.; width: 3.1-3.4 cm.; height: 2.3 cm.
1st century C.E.
Burial 1, burial ground near Kosika village, Enotaev region, Astrakhan oblast
Astrakhan Historic Architectural Museum
Inventory number KP 35529

Cat. 9

Cat. 10. Ornaments from a harness. Four pieces (Plate 31)

Openwork; boss in the center; loop on the back.
Gold. Cast, wire-drawn, soldered.
Diameter: 4.7 cm.; height (excluding loop): 1.3 cm.
1st century C.E.
Burial 1, burial ground near Kosika village, Enotaev region, Astrakhan oblast
Astrakhan Historic Architectural Museum
Inventory numbers KP 35603, 35604, 35605, 35606

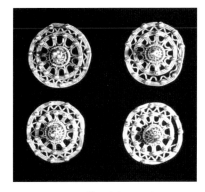

Cat.10

Cat. 11. Whetstone finial (Plate 32)

In the form of a predator head; flat stones (now lost) mounted in the ears and eyes; ring at the top for suspension.
Gold; greyish-yellowish-greenish stone of jade type. Ground, stamped.
Length: 21.2 cm.; width: 2.1 cm.
1st century C.E.
Burial 1, burial ground near Kosika village, Enotaev region, Astrakhan oblast
Astrakhan Historic Architectural Museum
Inventory number KP 40921

Cat. 11

Cat. 12. Finial for a bone object (Plate 33)

A cylinder with a plate soldered onto one end; decorated on the edges with two braided wires. Bone residual found inside.
Gold. Forged, hammered, wire-drawn, soldered.
Diameter: 1.7 cm.; height: 5.0 cm.
1st century B.C.E.
Burial 1, burial ground near Kosika village, Enotaev region, Astrakhan oblast
Astrakhan Historic Architectural Museum
Inventory number KP 40675

Cat. 13. Tongue of a belt (Plates 34, 35)

Two plates decorated with geometric designs; an aperture on one end for inserting one end of a leather belt and a prongs for fastening the plate to the other end.
Gold. Cast, wire-drawn, soldered, cloisonne.
1sst century C.E.
Length: 5.0 cm.; width: 1.4; cm. depth: 0.4 cm.
Burial 1, burial ground near Kosika village, Enotaev region, Astrakhan oblast
Astrakhan Historic Architectural Museum
Inventory number KP 35538

Cat. 12

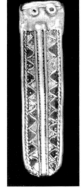

Cat. 13

Cat. 14. Finial, zoomorphic form (Plate 36)

In the form of a horse head or wolf head; end soldered in place. Formerly had stone or colored glass inlays and was attached with nails.
Gold, colored glass or stones. Forged, soldered, stamped, inlaid.
Length: 4.3 cm.; width: 11.0 cm.
1st century C.E.
Burial 1, burial ground near Kosika village, Enotaev region, Astrakhan oblast
Astrakhan Historic Architectural Museum
Inventory number KP 35538

Cat. 14

Cat. 15. Stone effigy of a man (Plate 37)

A bust with crudely carved face and hands. Appears badly weathered.
Sandstone. Carved.
Height 70.0 cm.; width: 32.0 cm.
6th-7th centuries C.E.
Origin unknown.
Astrakhan Historic Architectural Museum
Inventory number PA 25367

Cat. 15

Cat.16. Plate (Plate 38)
Flat bottom without base. Broad, flaring rim. A coat of arms in the center is encircled by friezes depicting scenes of paired animals attacking each other. Frieze on rim is of single animals alternating with foliate scrollwork and surrounded by a scalloped grapevine motif. Italian craftsmanship.
Silver gilt. Cast, chased, engraved.
Diameter: 23.6 cm.; height: 5.0 cm.
14th century C.E.
Burial ground near the village Belorechensk, Maikop, Kuban oblast (now Krasnodar krai)
State Hermitage.
Inventory number Kub 991

Cat. 16

Cat. 17. Coins (200 specimens, Plate 39)
Part of a hoard of Golden Horde dirhams.
Hidden ca.1395.
Silver. Striking.
Maximum diameter of each coin: 1.4-1.5 cm.
14th century
Karatun village, Apastov region, Tatarstan.
National Local Lore Center of Tatarstan, Kazan.
Inventory number Kub 4327

Cat. 17

Cat. 18. Dinar (obverse) (Plates 40, 41)
One of the coins of Mahmoud, Sultan of Delhi.
Gold. Striking.
Diameter: 2.0 cm.; depth: 0.2 cm.
1316/1317 C.E.
Treasure of Simferopol, Krym oblast (Crimea), Ukraine
State Historical Museum, Moscow
Inventory number 99264-2

Cat. 18

Cat. 19. Dinar (reverse) (Plates 42, 43)
One of the coins of Mahmoud, Sultan of Delhi.
Gold. Striking.
Diameter: 2.0 cm.; depth: 0.2 cm.
1351/1352 C.E.
Treasure of Simferopol, Krym oblast (Crimea), Ukraine
State Historical Museum, Moscow
Inventory number 99264-3

Cat. 19

Cat. 20. Set of belt ornaments, 10 pieces (Plates 44, 45)
Finial and plaques with holes for attaching onto a leather belt; decorated with rosettes and birds.
Gold. Cast, engraving, niello.
Length of the tongue: 4.8 cm.; length of plaques: 2.2; cm. diameter of round plaque: 2.0 cm.
14th century C.E.
Treasure of Simferopol, Krym oblast (Crimea), Ukraine
Possibly Italian workmanship.
State Historical Museum, Moscow
Inventory number 99264-8

Cat. 20

Cat. 21. Set of belt ornaments, 11 objects (Plates 46-48)
Buckle, tongue, and plaques with geometric and floral designs originally attached with prongs to a belt, undoubtedly made of leather.
Silver. Casting, engraving, enamel.
Length of buckle: 10.1 cm.; length of tongue: 12.1 cm.; width: 2.1 cm.
14th century C.E.
Treasure of Simferopol', Krym oblast (Crimea), Ukraine
Possibly Italian workmanship.
State Historical Museum, Moscow
Inventory number 99264-5

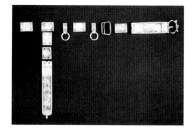

Cat. 21

Cat. 22. Set of belt ornaments, 28 pieces (Plates 49 and 50)
Open-work plaques with floral and geometric motifs; large ornamental plaques with carnelian inlays; all formerly attached to a belt with prongs. Gold, carnelian.
Casting, engraving, inlay.
Length of plaque with loop: 6.5, cm. 3.4 cm.; length of tongue with hook: 12.4 cm., 2.1 cm.
14th century C.E.
Treasure of Simferopol, Krym oblast (Crimea), Ukraine
State Historical Museum, Moscow
Inventory number 99264-12

Cat. 22

Cat. 23. Bracelet (Plate 51)
Composed of ornamented square and rectangular plaques; rectangular plaques display columns terminating in animal snouts that flank a Persian inscription: "Let the Creator be a patron of the owner of this, wherever he goes." One plaque has a tang for fastening the bracelet and a loop for suspending an object, now lost.
Gold. Casting, wire-drawing, soldering, chasing, engraving, inlay, niello.
Length: 13.9 cm.; width: 1.8 cm.
14th century C.E.
Treasure of Simferopol, Krym oblast (Crimea), Ukraine
State Historical Museum, Moscow
Inventory number 99264 -18

Cat. 23

Cat. 24. Bracelet (Plate 52)

Bent rod terminating with the heads of fantastic creatures. Pastiche.
Gold, cast.
14th century C.E.
Maximum diameter: 11.0 cm.; Depth: 0.4 cm.
Treasure of Simferopol, Krym oblast (Crimea), Ukraine
State Historical Museum, Moscow
Inventory number 99264-17

Cat. 24

Cat. 25. Chain for a headdress (Plate 53)

Consists of 16 round links, each with an inset pearl or carnelian;
hook on one end for attaching; opposite end may be lost.
Gold, pearls, turquoise. Cast, inlaid, granulation.
Diameter of round links: 1.5 cm.; length: 38.0 cm.
14th century C.E.
Treasure of Simferopol, Krym oblast (Crimea), Ukraine
State Historical Museum, Moscow
Inventory number 99264-25

Cat. 25

Cat. 26. Plaques. 3 pieces (Plate 54)

Open-work plaques. Each has a setting in the center for an inlay,
now lost. To be sewn on clothing.
Gold, carnelian, amethyst. Cast, inlaid, filigree, granulation.
Width: 2.7 cm.; Depth: 0.3 cm.
14th century C.E.
Treasure of Simferopol, Krym oblast (Crimea), Ukraine
State Historical Museum, Moscow
Inventory number 99264-20

Cat. 26

Cat. 27. Plaque from a headdress (Plate 55)

Round plaque decorated with small stone inlays surrounding a large
central inlay. Originally attached to a headdress.
Gold, turquoise, amethyst. Cast, inlaid, granulation.
Diameter: 3.5 cm.; height: 1.1 cm.
14th century C.E.
Treasure of Simferopol, Krym oblast (Crimea), Ukraine
State Historical Museum, Moscow
Inventory number 99264-27

Cat. 27

Cat. 28. P'ai-tzü (symbol of authority) (Plates 56, 57)

Oval tablet; molded hole toward one end used for suspension. The
sun and moon are depicted above the hole; below a vertical Mongol
inscription written in Uighur script: "By the power of eternal
Heaven and by the protection of the great might and radiance. An
edict of Keldibeg. Any person who does not respect [this] shall be
slain and die."
Silver gilt. Cast, engraved.
Length: 29.8 cm.; width: 9.7; Depth: 0.6 cm.
1361/1362 C.E.
Treasure of Simferopol, Krym oblast (Crimea), Ukraine
State Historical Museum, Moscow
Inventory number 99264-1

Cat. 28

Cat. 29. Divination bowl (Plates 58, 59)
Spherical, without base. On both sides, distorted Arabic letters; on the exterior, a stylized human face represented as if it were the sun.
Silver. Cast, engraving.
Diameter: 10.9 cm.; height: 2.6 cm.
14th century C.E.
Treasure of Simferopol, Krym oblast (Crimea), Ukraine
State Historical Museum, Moscow
Inventory number 99264-13

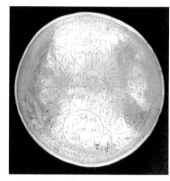

Cat. 29

Cat. 30. Ladle (Plates 60 and 61)
The finial on the long ladle handle is of a sitting figure of a man wearing a pointed cap, drinking from the vessel he holds with both hands. An eagle-owl image decorates the junction of ladle and handle.
Silver. Cast.
Diameter: 25.8 cm.; width of the ladle: 8.6 cm.
14th century C.E.
Treasure of Simferopol, Krym oblast (Crimea), Ukraine
State Historical Museum, Moscow
Inventory number 99264-26

Cat. 30

Cat. 31. Case for prayer texts (Plate 62)
A sub-triangular shaped box decorated with scrollwork and the "knot of happiness."
Gold. Forging, soldering, filigree.
Length: 6.6 cm.; width: 6.5; Depth: 1.0 cm.
14th century C.E.
Treasure of Simferopol, Krym oblast (Crimea), Ukraine
State Historical Museum, Moscow
Inventory number 99264-21

Cat.31

Cat. 32. Case for prayer texts (Plate 63, right)
An open-work, cylindrical box with loops for suspension; elaborate ornamentation and inscription.
Gold. Forged, soldered, filigree.
Length: 6.0 cm.; width: 3.2 cm.
14th century C.E.
Treasure of Simferopol, Krym oblast (Crimea), Ukraine
State Historical Museum, Moscow
Inventory number 99264-29

Cat. 32

Cat. 33. Case for prayer texts (Plate 63, left)
An-open work, cylindrical box with loops for suspension; elaborate ornamentation and inscription.
Gold. Forging, soldering, filigree.
Length: 6.1 cm.; width: 3.2 cm.
14th century C.E.
Treasure of Simferopol, Krym oblast (Crimea), Ukraine
State Historical Museum, Moscow
Inventory number 99264-28

Cat. 33

Cat. 34. Set of belt ornaments. 10 pieces (Plate 64)

Buckles, tongues, and plaques with Chinese style ornamentation, originally attachments for a leather belt.
Gilt bronze. Forged, stamped.
Length of tongue: 8.0 cm.; width of tongue: 2.6 cm.; maximum dimension of plaques: 5.0 cm.
14th century C.E.
Selitrennoe, Kharabalin region, Astrakhan oblast
Department of Archaeology, Historical Faculty, Moscow State University
Inventory number 1989-12

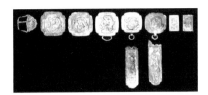
Cat. 34

Cat. 35. Fragment of a glass vessel, 4 pieces (Plate 65)

Fragments of a fine glass vessel; form cannot be reconstructed from the existing fragments.
Glass, enamel. blown, painted, fired.
Maximum dimension: 4.6 cm.
14th century C.E.
Selitrennoe, Kharabalin region, Astrakhan oblast
State Historical Museum, Moscow
Inventory number 2680–125–128

Cat. 35

Cat. 36. Fragment of a glass vessel (Plate 66)

Fragment of a flat bowl or a dish. Preserved painting reveals a medallion with cranes among plants and fruit.
Glass, enamel. Blowing, painting, firing.
Maximum dimension: 15.0 cm.
14th century C.E.
Selitrennoe, Kharabalin region, Astrakhan oblast
Astrakhan Historical Architectural Museum
Inventory number PO 1971-56

Cat. 36

Cat. 37. Fragment of mosaic (Plate 67, top)

Constructed of elements, each cut from flat tiles; each element has a distinct painted color that when assembled with others creates a geometric ornamentation. Kashi, lustreware; overglaze painting, fired.
Length: 15.0 cm.; width: 14.0 cm.; depth: 3.0 cm.
14th century C.E.
Selitrennoe, Kharabalin region, Astrakhan oblast
Astrakhan Historic Architectural Museum
Inventory number PO 1977-84

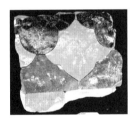
Cat. 37

Cat. 38. Fragment of a tile (Plate 67, bottom)

Flat tile decorated with a trefoil motif.
Kashi, lustreware; overglaze painting, fired.
Maximum dimension: 18.0 cm.; depth: 2.7 cm.
14th century C.E.
Selitrennoe, Kharabalin region, Astrakhan oblast
Astrakhan Historic Architectural Museum
Inventory number PO 1984-68

Cat. 38

Cat. 39. Fragment of a tile (Plate 68)

Flat tile with the depiction of a person wering a pointed hat or headdress; floral motif in the background.
Kashi, lustreware; overglaze painting, fired.
Maximum dimension: 7.0 cm.; depth: 2.7 cm.
14th century C.E.
Selitrennoe, Kharabalin region, Astrakhan oblast
State Museum of Oriental Art, Moscow
Inventory number GMV–4380

Cat. 39

Cat. 40. Fragment of a tile panel (Plate 69)

Combined star- and hexagon-shaped tiles with geometric design. A Persian inscription runs along the edge of the star-shaped fragment: ". . . poems. Oh, be a seal of universal beauty on my soul. And in my soul. . . ."
Kashi, lustreware; overglaze painting, fired.
Maximum dimension: 14.7 cm.; sides of the hexagonal tile: 3.8 cm.; depth: 2.7 cm.
14th century C.E.
Selitrennoe, Kharabalin region, Astrakhan oblast
Astrakhan Historic Architectural Museum
Inventory number PO–1977–90

Cat. 40

Cat. 41. Fragments of a tile panel (9 pieces, Plate 70)

Flat star- and irregular polygon-shaped elements, decorated with floral and geometric motifs; originally a part of the decoration in the central hall of a large house at Selitrennoe.
Kashi, lustreware; overglaze painting, fired.
Maximum dimension of the largest fragment: 13.1 cm.; depth: 2.8 cm.
14th century C.E.
Selitrennoe, Kharabalin region, Astrakhan oblast
State Historical Museum, Moscow
Inventory number 2671-10.25

Cat. 41

Cat. 42. Fragments of a tile (3 objects, Plate 71)

Flat sub-rectangular tiles with a floral motif. Originally used in a border composition decorating the same hall as that illustrated in Catalogue 41.
Kashi, lustreware; overglaze painting, fired.
Maximum dimension: 15.2 cm.; depth: 2.7 cm.
14th century C.E.
Selitrennoe, Kharabalin region, Astrakhan oblast
Astrakhan Historic Architectural Museum
Inventory number PO 1977-87-89

Cat. 42

Cat. 43. Fragment of mosaic (Plate 72)

Constructed from pieces cut from flat tiles. Each element is a distinct color and together they make up a floral motif.
Length: 35 cm.; width: 18.0 cm.; depth: 2.7 cm.
Kashi, lustreware; overglaze painting, fired.
14th century C.E.
Selitrennoe, Kharabalinskii region, Astrakhanskai oblast
State Historical Museum, Moscow
Inventory number 2080-136

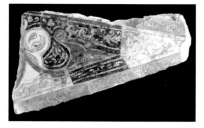

Cat. 43

Cat. 44. Fragment of a tile (Plate 73)

Flat tile decorated with interlace, flowers, and scrolls.
Kashi, lustreware; overglaze painting, fired.
Length: 21.0 cm.; width: 13.0 cm.; depth: 2.8 cm.
14th century C.E.
Selitrennoe, Kharabalin region, Astrakhan oblast
State Historical Museum, Moscow
Inventory number 2693-43

Cat. 44

Cat. 45. Tile (Plate 74, left)

Flat tile with incised interlace motif.
Terracotta. Engraved, fired.
Height: 13.5 cm.; width: 7.5 cm.; depth: 3.0 cm.
14th century C.E.
Selitrennoe, Kharabalin region, Astrakhan oblast
State Historical Museum, Moscow
Inventory number 2692-32

Cat. 45

Cat. 46. Tile (Plate 74, right)

Flat tile with an abstract geometric motif.
Kashi, lustreware; overglaze painting, fired.
Maximum dimension: 19.5 cm.; width: 2.7; depth: 3.0 cm.
14th century C.E.
Selitrennoe, Kharabalin region, Astrakhan oblast
State Historical Museum, Moscow
Inventory number 2678-57

Cat. 46

Cat. 47. Tile (Plate 75)

Flat tile with abstract and floral motif; the abstracted motif may be
elements of Kufic inscription.
Kashi, lustreware; overglaze painting, fired.
Maximum dimension: 19.0 cm.; depth: 2.8 cm.
14th century C.E.
Selitrennoe, Kharabalin region, Astrakhan oblast
State Historical Museum, Moscow
Inventory number 2692-6

Cat. 47

Cat. 48. Fragment of a tile (Plate 76, top)

Flat tile with abstract floral motif that may be elements of a Kufic
inscription.
Kashi, lustreware; overglaze painting, fired.
Maximum dimension: 12.0 cm.; depth: 3.0 cm.
14th century C.E.
Selitrennoe, Kharabalin region, Astrakhan oblast
Astrakhan Historic Architectural Museum
Inventory number PO–1983–21

Cat. 48

Cat. 49. Fragment of a tile (Plate 76, bottom)

Flat tile with floral motif.
Kashi, lustreware; overglaze painting, fired.
Maximum dimension: 12.0 cm.; depth: 3.0 cm.
14th century C.E.
Selitrennoe, Kharabalin region, Astrakhan oblast
Astrakhan Historic Architectural Museum
Inventory number PO–1982–6

Cat. 49

Cat. 50. Fragments of a tile, 2 objects (Plate 77)

Flat tiles with geometric design inside heart-shaped motif; originally part of a decorative panel.
Kashi, lustreware; overglaze painting, fired.
Maximum dimension: 5.5 cm.; depth: 3.0 cm.
14th century C.E.
Selitrennoe, Kharabalin region, Astrakhan oblast
Astrakhan Historic Architectural Museum
Inventory number PO–1983–11, 12

Cat. 50

Cat. 51. Fragment of a tile (Plate 78)

Flat tile with Persian inscription: "Master wonderful. . . ."
Kashi, lustreware; overglaze painting, fired.
Maximum dimension: 18.0 cm.; width: 12.5 cm.; depth: 2.7 cm.
14th century C.E.
Selitrennoe, Kharabalin region, Astrakhan oblast
Astrakhan Historic Architectural Museum
Inventory number PO–1985–9

Cat. 51

Cat. 52. Tile panel (Plate 79)

Assembled from fragments and complete tiles forming floral and geometric designs. Originally belonged to the decor of the same house as noted in Catalogue Nos. 41 and 42.
Kashi, lustreware; overglaze painting, fired.
Length: 70.0 cm.; width: 50.0 cm.
14th century C.E.
Selitrennoe, Kharabalin region, Astrakhan oblast
Astrakhan Historic Architectural Museum
Inventory number PO–1977–4

Cat. 52

Cat. 53. Mosaic panel (Plate 80)

Round medallion constructed as single element from flat tiles; seven rosettes in the center. Persian inscription around the edge: "The world is bound to the will of fate, and the king is the shepherd, and hope lives, and a strong state, and the luck of a young man."
Kashi, glaze. Carved and fired.
Diameter: 145.0 cm.; depth: 3.0 cm.
14th century C.E.
Selitrennoe, Kharabalin region, Astrakhan oblast
Astrakhan Historic Architectural Museum
Inventory number PO–1980–1

Cat. 53

Cat. 54. Architectural element (Plate 81)
Octagonal tile with geometric ornament in relief.
Terracotta; molded, glazed, fired.
Maximum dimension: 32.2 cm.; depth: 4.0 cm.
14th century C.E.
Selitrennoe, Kharabalin region, Astrakhan oblast
State Historical Museum, Moscow
Inventory number 2692—15

Cat. 54

Cat. 55. Fragments of window grills. 5 objects (Plate 82)
Flat open-work window grills; clear and colored glass pieces were
glued to the back of the grills.
Alabaster, casting, carving.
Maximum dimension of largest fragment: 13.0 cm.; depth: 3.0 cm.
14th century C.E.
Selitrennoe, Kharabalin region, Astrakhan oblast
State Historical Museum, Moscow
Inventory number 2691–30–33

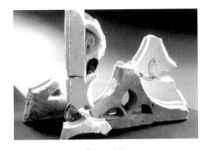

Cat. 55

Cat. 56. Bowl (Plate 83)
Hemispherical bowl with a ring base; centaur in low relief painted
on the interior center; geometric and stylized floral motifs in the
background.
Kashi, glaze. Wheel-thrown, molded; underglaze painted, fired.
Diameter: 22.0 cm.; height: 8.0 cm.
14th century C.E.
Selitrennoe, Kharabalin region, Astrakhan oblast
Astrakhan Historic Architectural Museum
Inventory number KP–243546

Cat. 56

Cat. 57. Fragment of a bowl (Plate 84)
Hemispherical bowl with a ring base; two waterfowl painted and in
low relief.
Kashi, glaze. Wheel-thrown, molded decoration, underglaze
painting, fired.
Maximum dimension: 15.0 cm.
14th century C.E.
Selitrennoe, Kharabalin region, Astrakhan oblast
Astrakhan Historic Architectural Museum
Inventory number PO–1981–1

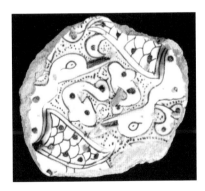

Cat. 57

Cat. 58. Fragment of a bowl (Plate 85)

Hemispherical bowl with a ring base; two waterfowl painted in low relief.
Kashi, glaze. Wheel-thrown, molded decoration, underglaze painting, fired.
Maximum dimension: 16.0 cm.
14th century C.E.
Selitrennoe, Kharabalin region, Astrakhan oblast
State Historical Musuem, Moscow
Inventory number 2692–5

Cat. 58

Cat. 59. Bowl (Plate 86)

Flat bowl with a ring base; smooth surface; floral decoration painted radially between bands.
Kashi, glaze. Molding, potter's wheel, underglaze painting, firing.
Diameter: 23.0 cm.; height: 9.0 cm.
14th century C.E.
Selitrennoe, Kharabalin region, Astrakhans oblast
Astrakhan Historic Architectural Museum
Inventory number PO–1987–15

Cat. 60. Bowl (Plate 87, upper left)

Shallow bowl with a ring base; geometric and floral decoration in low relief.
Kashi, glaze. Wheel-thrown, molded decoration, underglaze painting, fired.
Diameter: 20.0 cm.; height: 7.1 cm.
14th century C.E.
Selitrennoe, Kharabalin region, Astrakhan oblast
Astrakhan Historic Architectural Museum
Inventory number PO–1983–160

Cat. 59

Cat. 61. Fragment of a bowl (Plate 87, lower left)

Deep bowl with a ring base; smooth surface; lotus flower motif on the interior with geometric band at rim.
Kashi, glaze. Wheel-thrown, molded decoration, underglaze painting, fired.
Maximum dimension: 9.0 cm.
14th century C.E.
Selitrennoe, Kharabalin region, Astrakhan oblast
Astrakhan Historic Architectural Museum
Inventory number PO–1987–15

Cat. 62. Fragment of a bowl (Plate 87, right)

Shallow bowl with a ring base; smooth surface; stylized lotus in center; geometricized floral motif on interior sidewalls; rim lost.
Kashi, glaze. Wheel-thrown, molded decoration, underglaze painting, fired.
Maximum dimension: 15.0 cm.
14th century C.E.
Selitrennoe, Kharabalin region, Astrakhan oblast
Astrakhan Historic Architectural Museum
Inventory number PO–1988–6

Cat. 60-62

Cat. 63. Bowl (Plate 88, left)
Shallow bowl with a ring base; stylized lotus in relief within medallions; wheel motif in interior center.
Kashi, glaze. Wheel-thrown, molded decoration, underglaze painting, fired.
Diameter: 21.0 cm.; height: 6.9 cm.
14th century C.E.
Selitrennoe, Kharabalin region, Astrakhan oblast
Astrakhan Historic Architectural Museum
Inventory number PO–1981–32

Cat. 63, 64

Cat. 64. Bowl (Plate 88, right)
Small, deep bowl with a ring base; exterior center, six-petaled rosette surrounded by geometric motif on the sides.
Kashi, glaze. Wheel-thrown, molded decoration, underglaze painting, fired.
Diameter: 15.5 cm.; height: 7.0 cm.
14th century C.E.
Selitrennoe, Kharabalin region, Astrakhan oblast
Astrakhan Historic Architectural Museum
Inventory number PO–1978–19

Cat. 65. Misfired bowl (Plate 89, left)
Bowl with ring base; decorated with stylized herringbone design. Tilobed support used during firing has fallen into the bowl and adhered to the glaze.
Kashi, glaze. Wheel-thrown, molded decoration, underglaze painting, fired.
Diameter: 22.0 cm.; height: 6.0 cm.
14th century C.E.
Selitrennoe, Kharabalin region, Astrakhan oblast
Astrakhan Historic Architectural Museum
Inventory number PO–1977–15

Cat. 65, 66

Cat. 66. Bowl (Plate 89, center)
Bowl with ring base; three-petal rosette painted on the interior center.
Clay, engobe, glaze. Wheel-thrown, engraved, fired.
Diameter: 23.0 cm.; height: 7.8.0 cm.
14th century C.E.
Selitrennoe, Kharabalin region, Astrakhan oblast
Astrakhan Historic Architectural Museum
Inventory number PO–1978–23

Cat. 67. Bowl (Plate 89, right)
Hemispherical bowl with ring base; geometric design of radiating stripes, alternating solid color and geometric design; bowl misshapend during firing.
Kashi, glaze. Wheel-thrown, molded decoration, underglaze painting, fired.
Diameter: 16.0 cm.; height: 6.0 cm.
14th century C.E.
Selitrennoe, Kharabalin region, Astrakhan oblast
Astrakhan Historic Architectural Museum
Inventory number PO–1979–41

Cat. 67

Cat. 68. Bowl (Plate 90, left)
Shallow bowl with ring base; elaborate rosette painted on interior center; floral and geometric motifs below rim.
Kashi, glaze. Wheel-thrown, molded decoration, underglaze painting, fired.
Diameter: 22.0 cm.; height: 10.0 cm.
14th century C.E.
Selitrennoe, Kharabalin region, Astrakhan oblast
State Historical Museum, Moscow
Inventory number 2672–457

Cat. 69. Bowl (Plate 90, center)
Deep bowl with a ring base; relief surface has a floral design; one word Arabic inscription repeats below the interior rim: "Success." Arcade pattern decorates the exterior surface.
Kashi, glaze. Wheel-thrown, molded decoration, underglaze painting, fired.
Diameter: 21.0 cm.; height: 8.1 cm.
14th century C.E.
Selitrennoe, Kharabalin region, Astrakhan oblast
State Historical Museum, Moscow
Inventory number 2692–21

Cat. 68-70

Cat. 70. Bowl (Plate 90, right)
Deep bowl with ring base; rosette in the center surrounded by an undecorated and then geometric band; crosshatching below rim.
Kashi, glaze. Wheel-thrown, molded decoration, underglaze painting, fired.
Diameter: 15.5 cm.; height: 6.0 cm.
14th century C.E.
Selitrennoe, Kharabalin region, Astrakhan oblast
State Historical Museum, Moscow
Inventory number 2693–16

Cat. 71. Bowl (Plate 91, left)

Deep bowl with a ring base; glazed to imitate Chinese celadon.
Kashi, glaze. Wheel-thrown, molded, fired.
Diameter: 10.0 cm.; height: 5.3 cm.
14th century C.E.
Selitrennoe, Kharabalin region, Astrakhan oblast
State Historical Museum, Moscow
Inventory number 2692–7

Cat. 71, 72

Cat. 72. Bowl (Plate 91, right)

Deep bowl with a ring base; six-pointed star on interior center; six
pointed leaves placed between the rays of the star.
Clay, engobe, glaze. Wheel-thrown, engraved, fired.
Diameter: 11.4 cm.; height: 6.0 cm.
14th century C.E.
Selitrennoe, Kharabalin region, Astrakhan oblast
State Historical Museum, Moscow
Inventory number 2692–11

Cat. 73. Bowl (Plate 92, left)

Shallow bowl with ring base; six-pointed star with lotus on the
interior center; two registers of geometric ornamentation above
center decoration.
Kashi, glaze. Wheel-thrown, molded, underglaze painted, fired.
Diameter: 17.0 cm.; height: 7.8 cm.
14th century C.E.
Selitrennoe, Kharabalin region, Astrakhan oblast
State Historical Museum, Moscow
Inventory number 2693–7

Cat. 73, 74

Cat. 74. Bowl (Plate 92, right)

Deep bowl with ring base; relief decoration on the interior, floral
motif surrounded by rows of geometric design; arches decorate the
exterior surface.
Kashi, glaze. Wheel-thrown, molded, underglaze painted, fired.
Diameter: 15; height: 7.2 cm.
14th century C.E.
Selitrennoe, Kharabalin region, Astrakhan oblast
State Historical Museum, Moscow
Inventory number 2691–23

Cat. 75. Fragments of vase (2 pieces, Plate 93)

Thick walls, relief surface; decorated with a polo scene. The form of
the vase cannot be reconstructed from the surviving fragments.
Kashi, glaze. Wheel-thrown, molded, fired.
Maximum dimension of the largest fragment: 23.0 cm.; depth: 1.4
cm.
14th century C.E.
Selitrennoe, Kharabalin region, Astrakhan oblast
State Historical Museum, Moscow
Inventory number 2676–28

Cat. 75

Cat. 76. Vessel (Plate 94, left)

Vase with bulbous sides, steep shoulders closing to smaller and narrow upstanding rim; ring base; vertical lines in relief. Celedon glazed. Made in China.
White clay, porcelain type. Wheel-thrown, molded, glazed; fired.
Diameter: 6.5 cm.; height: 6.5 cm.
14th century C.E.
Selitrennoe, Kharabalin region, Astrakhan oblast
State Historical Museum, Moscow
Inventory number 2671–47

Cat 76

Cat. 77. Pile of misfired bowls, three objects (Plate 94, right)

Deep bowls with ring bases. Vertical relief lines on the body in imitation of Chinese Celadon glazed vessels. Adhered together with molten glaze during firing.
Kashi, glaze. Wheel-thrown, molded, glazed, fired.
Diameter: 6.6 cm.; height: 12.1 cm.
14th century C.E.
Selitrennoe, Kharabalin region, Astrakhan oblast
State Historical Museum, Moscow
Inventory number 2692–8

Cat. 77

Cat. 78. Bowl (Plate 95)

Shallow bowl with ring base. Depiction of flying bird surrounded by floral motifs. Imitation Chinese porcelain.
Kashi, glaze. Wheel-thrown, molded, underglaze painted, fired.
Diameter: 25 cm.; height: 10.0 cm.
14th century C.E.
Selitrennoe, Kharabalin region, Astrakhan oblast
State Historical Museum, Moscow
Inventory number 2694–13

Cat. 78

Cat. 79. Fragment of a bowl (Plate 96)
Bowl with ring base. Depiction of flying bird surrounded by floral motifs. Imitation Chinese porcelain.
Kashi, glaze. Molding, potter's wheel, underglaze painting, firing.
Maximum dimension: 17.0 cm.
14th century C.E.
Selitrennoe, Kharabalin region, Astrakhan oblast
State Historical Museum, Moscow
Inventory number 2694–14

Cat. 79

Cat. 80. Fragment of a bowl (Plate 97, top)
Bowl with ring base. Depiction of flying bird surrounded by floral motifs. Imitation Chinese porcelain.
Kashi, glaze. Molding, potter's wheel, underglaze painting, firing.
Maximum dimension: 10.0 cm.
14th century C.E.
Selitrennoe, Kharabalin region, Astrakhan oblast
State Historical Museum, Moscow
Inventory number 2693–17

Cat. 80

Cat. 81. Fragment of bowl (Plate 97, center left)
Bowl; form unreconstructed. Painted depiction of a bird's head.
Clay, engobe, glaze. Wheel-thrown, engraved, fired.
Maximum dimension: 3.5 cm.
14th century C.E.
Selitrennoe, Kharabalin region, Astrakhan oblast
State Historical Museum, Moscow
Inventory number 2693–19

Cat. 81

Cat. 82. Fragment of vessel (Plate 97, bottom)
Neck of a vessel; depiction of a bird among a floral motif.
Kashi, glaze. Wheel-thrown, molded decoration, underglaze painting, fired.
Maximum dimension: 12.0 cm.
14th century C.E.
Selitrennoe, Kharabalin region, Astrakhan oblast
State Historical Museum, Moscow
Inventory number 2672–46

Cat. 82

Cat. 83. Bowl (Plate 98)

Deep bowl with ring base and flared rim. Net pattern in the center; at the rim, a register of floral motifs alternated with an undecorated register; floral in the center; arches with floral motif around the exterior. Imitation of Chinese porcelain.
Kashi, glaze. Molding, potter's wheel, underglaze painting, firing.
Diameter: 23.0 cm.; height: 8.1 cm.
14th century C.E.
Selitrennoe, Kharabalin region, Astrakhan oblast
Astrakhan Historic Architectural Museum
Inventory number PO–1975–34

Cat. 83

Cat. 84. Fragment of vessel (Plate 99)

Fragment of a bottle; smooth surface, floral motif alternated with more realistic plants. Imitation of Chinese porcelain.
Kashi, glaze. Molding, potter's wheel, underglaze painting, firing.
Diameter: 10.0 cm.; height 17.0 cm.
14th century C.E.
Selitrennoe, Kharabalin region, Astrakhan oblast
Astrakhan Historic Architectural Museum
Inventory number PO–1970–5

Cat. 84

Cat. 85. Fragment of a bowl (Plate 100, top)

Sherd, smooth surface, decorated with alternate undecorated and floral bands. Imitation Chinese porcelain. The form of the bowl cannot be reconstructed from the existing fragment.
Kashi, glaze. Molding, potter's wheel, underglaze painting, firing.
Maximum dimension: 7.9 cm.
14th century C.E.
Selitrennoe, Kharabalin region, Astrakhan oblast
State Historical Museum, Moscow
Inventory number 2667–183

Cat. 85

Cat. 86. Fragment of a bowl (Plate 100, bottom)

Sherd, smooth surface decorated with geometric design. The form of the bowl can not be reconstructed from the existing fragment.
Kashi, glaze. Molding, potter's wheel, underglaze painting, firing.
Maximum dimension: 6.1 cm.
14th century C.E.
Selitrennoe, Kharabalin region, Astrakhan oblast
State Historical Museum, Moscow
Inventory number 2672–12

Cat. 86

Cat. 87. Bowl (Plate 101)

Biconical bowl with ring base. Upper frieze, a Persian inscription:
"They say there is water of life in the world. . . ." Four lower bands:
undecorated, geometric, floral, and undecorated.
Kashi, glaze. Wheel-thrown, molded decoration, underglaze
painting, fired.
Diameter: 21.0 cm.; height: 10.2 cm.
14th century C.E.
Selitrennoe, Kharabalin region, Astrakhan oblast
Astrakhan Historic Architectural Museum
Inventory number PO–1979–26

Cat. 87

Cat. 88. Fragment of a bowl (Plate 102)

Hemispherical bowl with ring base. Incised four-petaled floral motif,
possibly a Tree of Life, in the interior; scrolls between the petals.
Clay, engobe, glaze. Wheel-thrown, engraved, fired.
Maximum dimension: 19.7 cm.
14th century C.E.
Selitrennoe, Kharabalin region, Astrakhan oblast
State Historical Museum, Moscow
Inventory number 2692–149

Cat. 88

Cat. 89. Bowl (Plate 103, left)

Hemispherical bowl with undecorated smooth surface.
Clay, engobe, glaze. Wheel-thrown, fired.
Diameter: 11.0 cm.; height: 5.0 cm.
14th century C.E.
Selitrennoe, Kharabalinskii region, Astrakhanskaia oblast
Astrakhan Historic Architectural Museum
Inventory number PO–1979–29

Cat. 90. Bowl (Plate 103, center)

Hemispherical bowl with ring base. Geometric designs alternating
with undecorated bands radiating outward from center.
Clay, engobe, glaze. Wheel-thrown, molded, underglazed painted,
fired.
Diameter: 13.0 cm.; height: 5.2 cm.
14th century C.E.
Selitrennoe, Kharabalin region, Astrakhan oblast
Astrakhan Historic Architectural Museum
Inventory number PO–1980–4

Cat. 89-91

Cat. 91. Pitcher (Plate 103, right)

Pitcher. Tall, narrow neck, spout, flat bottom, handle oval in section.
Clay. Wheel-thrown, fired.
Diameter: 12.0 cm.; height: 20.0 cm.
14th century C.E.
Selitrennoe, Kharabalin region, Astrakhan oblast
Astrakhan Historic Architectural Museum
Inventory number PO–1981–16

Cat. 92. Money box (Plate 104, left)

Spherical body, narrows sharply toward flat bottom; slit for coins on the side.
Clay. Wheel-thrown, fired.
Diameter: 7.9 cm.; height: 7.6 cm.
14th century C.E.
Selitrennoe, Kharabalin region, Astrakhan oblast
State Historical Museum, Moscow
Inventory number 2692–240

Cats. 92-94

Cat. 93. Money-box (Plate 104, second from left)

Spherical body; narrows sharply toward a flat bottom; slit for coins on the side.
Clay. Wheel-thrown, fired.
Diameter: 9.9 cm.; height: 10.0 cm.
14th century C.E.
Selitrennoe, Kharabalin region, Astrakhan oblast
State Historical Museum, Moscow
Inventory number 2692–241

Cat. 94. Jug (ewer) (Plate 104, third from left)

Low, wide neck with incised ridges around body; unspouted; flat bottom; handle oval in section.
Clay. Wheel-thrown, fired.
Diameter: 12.7 cm.; height: 17.5 cm.
14th century C.E.
Selitrennoe, Kharabalin region, Astrakhan oblast
State Historical Museum, Moscow
Inventory number 2692—236

Cat. 95. Jug (ewer) (Plate 104, third from right)

Low short neck; flat bottom; unspouted; handle oval in section.
Clay. Wheel-thrown, fired.
Diameter: 7.0 cm.; height: 11.2 cm.
14th century C.E.
Selitrennoe, Kharabalin region, Astrakhan oblast
State Historical Museum, Moscow
Inventory number 2692–233

Cats. 95, 96

Cat. 96. Jug (ewer) (Plate 104, second from right)

Low short neck; flat bottom; unspouted; handle oval in section.
Clay. Wheel-thrown, fired.
Diameter: 7.1 cm.; height: 8.6 cm.
14th century C.E.
Selitrennoe, Kharabalin region, Astrakhan oblast
State Historical Museum, Moscow
Inventory number 2692–234

Cat. 97. Ewer (Plate 104, right)

Ewer with a short neck, flat bottom, handle oval in section; unspouted.
Clay. Wheel-thrown, fired.
Diameter: 10.8 cm.; height: 8.7 cm.
14th century C.E.
Selitrennoe, Kharabalin region, Astrakhan oblast
State Historical Museum, Moscow
Inventory number 2692–235

Cat. 97

Cat. 98. Fragment of misfired bowl (Plate 105)

Flat bowl with a ring base. Depiction of a stick-like person riding a fantastic bird or zoomorph.
Kashi, glaze. Molding, potter's wheel, underglaze painting, firing.
Diameter: 14.0 cm.
14th century C.E.
Selitrennoe, Kharabalin region, Astrakhan oblast
Astrakhan Historic Architectural Museum
Inventory number PO–1982–6

Cat. 98

Cat. 99. Amulet (Plate 106)

Oval plaque with Arabic inscription: "Set your hope on Allah Almighty."
Bronze. Cast, stamped.
Maximum dimension: 1.2 cm.; depth: 0.2 cm.
14th century C.E.
Selitrennoe, Kharabalin region, Astrakhan oblast
Department of Archaeology, Historical Faculty, Moscow State University.
Inventory number 1987–8

Cat 99

Cat. 100. Key (Plate 107, top, left)

Narrow, flat plate flaring toward the bottom; loop at the top, lower section bent.
Bronze. Forged.
Length: 3.9 cm.
14th century C.E.
Selitrennoe, Kharabalin region, Astrakhan oblast
State Historical Museum, Moscow
Inventory number 2692—23

Cat 100

Cat. 101. Small lock (Plate 107, top, right)

In the shape of a horse with interior mechanism. Hoop to be inserted in slits in the neck and crupper. Key hole on the side near front. Covered with compass ornaments.
Bronze. Soldering, engraving.
Length: 4.0 cm.; height: 5.0 cm.; depth: 0.9 cm.
14th century C.E.
Selitrennoe, Kharabalin region, Astrakhan oblast
State Historical Museum, Moscow
Inventory number 2694–13

Cat 101

Cat. 102. Plaque (Plate 107, second row, left)

In the form of a six-petaled rosette in relief.
Bronze. Cast.
Diameter: 2.0 cm.; depth: 0.5 cm.
14th century C.E.
Selitrennoe, Kharabalin region, Astrakhan oblast
State Historical Museum, Moscow
Inventory number 2692–37

Cat 102

Cat. 103. Weight (Plate 107, second row, center)

In the form of a flat, seven-petaled, unornamented rosette.
Bronze. Cast.
Diameter: 2.7 cm.; depth: 0.6 cm.
14th century C.E.
Selitrennoe, Kharabalin region, Astrakhan oblast
State Historical Museum, Moscow
Inventory number 2693–3

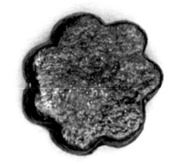

Cat 103

Cat. 104. Anvil for working jewelry (Plate 107, second row, right)

Faceted rod with a working surface on the top in the shape of polygon.
Bronze. Cast.
Height: 4.7 cm.; width: 2.1 cm.
14th century C.E.
Selitrennoe, Kharabalin region, Astrakhan oblast
State Historical Museum, Moscow
Inventory number 2692—23

Cat 104

Cat. 105. Support (Plate 107, third row, bottom)

Arc-shaped plate; marked in the center with a globe; ends rising and terminating with semi-spherical knobs. Vertical elements are decorated on the sides with schematicized animal heads.
Bronze. Cast.
Length: 8.1 cm.; height: 4.1 cm.
14th century C.E.
Selitrennoe, Kharabalinskii region, Astrakhanskaia oblast
State Historical Museum, Moscow
Inventory number 2692–7

Cat 105

Cat. 106. Weight (Plate 107, bottom, left)

Flat; polygon-shaped; possibly representing a rosette.
Bronze. Cast.
Diameter: 3.1 cm.; depth: 0.5 cm.
14th century C.E.
Selitrennoe, Kharabalin region, Astrakhan oblast
State Historical Museum, Moscow
Inventory number 2692–8

Cat 106

Cat. 107. Weight (Plate 107, lower row, right)

Flat, sub-semiglobular form.
Bronze. Cast.
 Diameter: 2.0 cm.; depth: 0.5 cm.
14th century C.E.
Selitrennoe, Kharabalin region, Astrakhan oblast
State Historical Museum, Moscow
Inventory number 2692–11

Cat 107

Cat. 108. Fastener (Plate 108, top, left)

Open ring with flattened ends extending outward; moveable tang across the ring. Knowns as a *sulgama*, used to fasten Mordvinian clothing.
Bronze. Cast, forged.
Height: 3.8 cm.
14th century C.E.
Selitrennoe, Kharabalin region, Astrakhan oblast
State Historical Museum, Moscow
Inventory number 2679–38

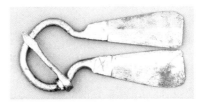

Cat 108

Cat. 109. Fastener (Plate 108, bottom, left)

Open ring with flattened ends extending outward. Known as a *sulgama*, used for fastening Mordvinian clothing.
Bronze. Cast, forged.
Height: 4.6 cm.
14th century C.E.
Selitrennoe, Kharabalin region, Astrakhan oblast
State Historical Museum, Moscow
Inventory number 2679–42

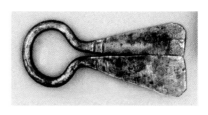

Cat 109

Cat. 110. Earring (Plate 108, center, left)

Open wire ring with a straight, elaborated shaft; wire is wound around the terminus of the shaft forming a cradle for a pearl.
Bronze, pearl, drawn wire.
Diameter: 2.2 cm.; height: 5.4 cm.
14th century C.E.
Selitrennoe, Kharabalin region, Astrakhan oblast
State Historical Museum, Moscow
Inventory number 2692–15

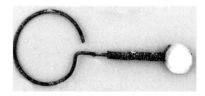

Cat 110

Cat. 111. Plaque (Plate 108, bottom, center)

Rectangular open-work plaque, ridged on one side; probably an attachment.
Bronze. Cast.
Length: 3.6 cm.; width: 2.4 cm.; depth: 0.4 cm.
14th century C.E.
Selitrennoe, Kharabalin region, Astrakhan oblast
Inventory number 2693–7

Cat 111

Cat. 112. Plaque (Plate 108, top, right)

In the form of an open-worked four-petaled rosette intended for attaching (sewn) on clothing.
Bone. Carved.
Width: 2.4 cm.; depth: 0.2 cm.
14th century C.E.
Selitrennoe, Kharabalin region, Astrakhan oblast
State Historical Museum, Moscow
Inventory number 2693–27

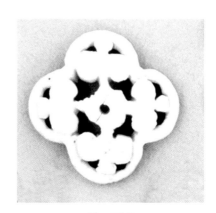

Cat 112

Cat. 113. Plaque (Plate 108, right)

Decorated with complex geometricized linear ornamentation. Function unknown.
Bronze. Forged, chased, engraved.
Width: 2.7 cm.; depth: 0.1 cm.
14th century C.E.
Selitrennoe, Kharabalin region, Astrakhan oblast
State Historical Museum, Moscow
Inventory number 2693-28

Cat 113

Cat. 114. Plaque (Plate 109, upper left)

Six-petaled rosette; filigree ornamentation within the petals, inset with stones; three metal strips in the center. Back is flat and undecorated.
Gold, lapis-lazuli. Cast, filigree.
Diameter: 1.8 cm.
14th century C.E.
Selitrennoe, Kharabalin region, Astrakhan oblast
Department of Archaeology, Historical Faculty, Moscow State University.
Inventory number 1989–16

Cat 114

Cat. 115. Plaque (Plate 109, bottom, left)

Flat rhombic plaque; embossed stylized rosette in center; holes for attachment (sewn) to clothing.
Gold. Stamped.
Maximum dimension: 1.0 cm.
14th century C.E.
Selitrennoe, Kharabalin region, Astrakhan oblast
Department of Archaeology, Historical Faculty, Moscow State University.
Inventory number 1987–322

Cat 115

Cat. 116. Plaque (Plate 109, right)

Thin rectangular plaque with interlaced floral motif in the center and a geometric register around the exterior; holes of attachment (sewn) to clothing.
Gold. Hammered, chased.
Length: 2; width: 1.3 cm.
14th century C.E.
Selitrennoe, Kharabalin region, Astrakhan oblast
Gold. Hammered, chased.
Department of Archaeology, Historical Faculty, Moscow State University.
Inventory number 1989–54

Cat 116

Appendix 1

Geneology of the Mongol Khagans, Khans, and Qatuns

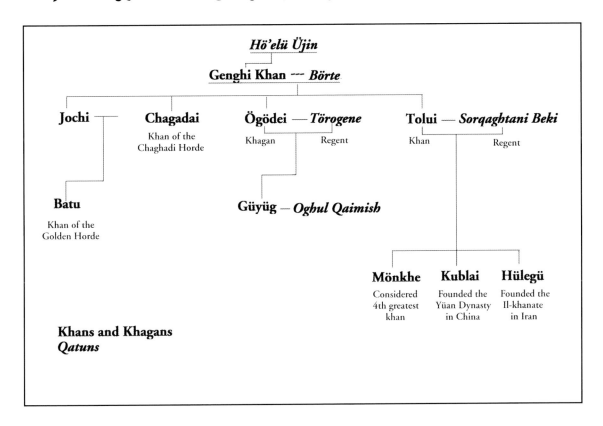

Hö'elü Üjin

Genghi Khan --- *Börte*

Jochi

Chagadai
Khan of the
Chaghadi Horde

Ögödei — *Törogene*
Khagan   Regent

Tolui — *Sorqaghtani Beki*
Khan   Regent

Batu
Khan of the
Golden Horde

Güyüg — *Oghul Qaimish*

Mönkhe
Considered
4th greatest
khan

Kublai
Founded the
Yüan Dynasty
in China

Hülegü
Founded the
Il-khanate
in Iran

Khans and Khagans
Qatuns

The geneology begins with Genghis Khan's mother. Quatuns (queens) noted here are those whose name have been recorded in texts. (ed. note)

The Glossary

Ahuramazda—supreme god of the ancient Iranian pantheon

aivan—large deep niche in the exterior of a building

Alania—Medieval country in the northern Caucasus, roughly coresponding to modern Ossetia.

Alans—people speaking an eastern Iranian language, descendants of the Sarmatians and progenitors of the modern Ossetians

Almalik—Medieval and modern city in Chinese Central Asia

Amazonia—mythical country of the Amazons in the Eurasian steppe

Aq-Kermen (Moncastro, Belgorod Dnestrovsk)–city of the Golden Horde period on the Dniester river

Arrigo, Lucino—Genovese merchant who traveled to Sarai in 1374

Ashina—ruling family in the Turkic khaganate

As—one of the Medieval names of the Alans-Ossetians.

Astrakhan—modern city on the lower Volga, built upon Hajji-tarkhan

Avars—nomadic people living on the steppes of eastern Europe in the middle of the 1st millennium C.E., and speaking a language possibly of the Turkic group

Avkhas—Medieval port on the Caucasus coast of the Black Sea

Azaq—Medieval city at the mouth of the Don, the predecessor of modern Azov

Bactria—ancient country in Central Asia. Parts of it are today in northern Afghanistan, southern Uzbekistan, and southern Tajikistan.

Batu—first khan of the Golden Horde, 1227—1255(?)

Belgorod Dnestrovskii—Russian name of Aq-Kermen (Moncastro)

Beljamen—city of the Golden Horde period in the Volga area

Belorechenskaia stanitsa—village on the Kuban river in the northern Caucasus

Berke—khan of the Golden Horde 1257—1267

Bohemia—Medieval kingdom of Czechia

bokka—ancient Mongolian female headdress, a cap with a vertical cylinder, topped with a horizontal board

Bolgar—main city of Volga Bulgaria

Bosporus—ancient kingdom in the Crimea and the Taman peninsula

Bukhara—Medieval and modern city in Central Asia, modern Uzbekistan

Caffa (Kaffa)—Medieval city in the Crimea, modern Feodosiya

caliph—title of the ruler of the Arab empire

caliphate—Arab empire; here, the Abbasid caliphate with its capital in Baghdad

Campanella, Tomazo—Italian writer and utopianist

capital—top section of a column

caravansary—stopping place for merchants and trading caravans

Celadon—type of Far Eastern porcelain with a pale green transluscent glaze

Chach—ancient name of the Tashkent oasis in modern Uzbekistan

Chaghatai—second son of Genghiz Khan

Ch'ang-ch'un—Taoist monk who travelled to Samarkand at the request of Genghiz Khan

Cherkess—group of tribes living in the northern Caucasus

Chernigov—Russian city

Chernyi Yar—site on the lower Volga

Chersonesus—ancient and Medieval city in the Crimea near modern Sevastopol

Chingizids—descendants of Genghiz Khan

Derbent—city and region on the Caucasian coast of the Caspian Sea

dinar—golden coin in the Islamic East

dirham—silver coin in the Islamic East

Dizabul—Turkic khagan

Dmitrii Ivanovich—Russian duke who defeated the Golden Horde Emir Mamay at Kulikov 1380

Dubovka—modern city near Volgograd

Dubrovnik (Raguza)—a port on the Adriatic Sea in modern Croatia

Dunhuang—area of the famous Buddhist religious complex in northwest China

Edel—name of the Volga on the map of Fra-Mauro (from the local name *Itil*)

Ektag—sacred mountain in Jety-su (Semirechiye), southern Kazakstan

emir—title of a leader in the Islamic East

Feodosiya—city in the Crimea (Medieval Caffa)

Fergana (also Ferghana)—ancient country in Central Asia in the Fergana valley; today the Fergana valley is divided between Uzbekistan, Tajikistan, and Kirghizstan

Gashun—burial site in the northern Caucasus

ger—round tent-like structure used by the Mongols, similar to the yurt (see yurt)

Girei Dynasty—rulers of the khanate of the Crimea; descendants of Jöchi

glaze—composition of materials covering the clay body of ceramics that when fired produces a glassy surface

Gog and Magog—tribes mentioned in Bible

Golden Mountain—Greek translation of the name Ektag

granulation—metallurgical technique in which small balls of metal, usually gold, are soldered to the surface of an object creating a decorative effect.

Gulistan—city of the Golden Horde whose location remains unknown

Güyük—grandson of Genghiz Khan, who became Great Khan of the Mongols from 1246 to 1248

Hajji-tarkhan—Medieval city in the Volga delta, the precursor of modern Astrakhan

Heraklea—Greek city

Hsiung-nu—confederacy who nomadized in the second half of the first millennium B.C.E. in Central Asia, and whose attacks upon the Chinese forced the Chinese to build the Great Wall. The Hsiung-nu migrated westward and arguably became the Huns.

Hsüan-tsang—Buddhist monk, famous for the description of his journey to the West

Huns—a nomadic confederacy originating in the East, and who in the 3rd and 4th centuries A.D. migrated to western Europe.

Ibn al-Athir—famous Arab historian of the thirteenth century

Il Khanids—Mongol (Chingizid) dynasty of Iran

imam—religious person in the Islamic East who leads prayers

incrustation—jewelry technique in which objects are decorated with bits of gemstones, glass, or precious metals

Itil—see Volga

Jand—Medieval city to the east of the Aral Sea

Janibeg—khan of the Golden Horde from 1348-1357

Jaroslav—duke of Suzdal

Genghiz Khan—founder of the Mongol Empire, 1206—1227

Jety-Su (Semirechiye)—ancient country in Central Asia that derives it name from seven rivers (although there are more than seven) located in the modern territory of southern Kazakhstan.

Jöchids—descendents of Jöchi, the eldest son of Genghiz Khan

Kalka—river where the united forces of Russians and Polovtsy were defeated by the Mongol army in 1223

kan—Chinese heating system of horizontal heating channels that run from the stove to the chimney under benches

Karakorum—Medieval city in Mongolia, the capital of the Mongol Empire.

karkhanah—large shop with many workers (Persian, "work house")

Kashghar—ancient oasis city in the Tarim Basin, Xinjiang Autonomous Region, Western China.

kashi—a special mixture of sand with clay and lime used as the body in the production of ceramic tiles and tableware

Kazaks—nomads living in the steppes of the northern Caucasus and the Volga and Don regions during the second half of the 1st millennium C.E. Today the Kazakhs have dispersed worldwide; the largest population lives a sedentary life in Kazakhstan while a large group still nomadize in western Mongolia.

Keldibeg—khan of the Mongol Horde in the period of anarchy (1357-1380) when more than twenty-five rival khans vied to be Great Khan.

Kerch—Medieval and modern city on the site of ancient Panticapeus, capital of the Bosporus Kingdom

khagan—Great Khan, title of a leader among the Old Turkic peoples and Mongols.

khan—title of a ruler in the Mongol empire

khatib—religious dignitary in the Islamic East

Khitans—Central Asian people who created a mighty empire but were destroyed by Genghiz Khan

Khotan—ancient city and oasis in the Tarim Basin, modern Xinjiang Autonomous Region of Western China.

Khwarizmshah Dynasty—rulers of a large empire centered in Khwarizm that was destroyed by the Mongols

Khwarizm—ancient oasis and country in the lower reaches of the Amu-Darya, Central Asia, now divided between Uzbekistan and Turkmenia

Kiev—capital of Old Russia, now capital of the Ukraine

Kiliya—city of the Golden Horde era on the Dnieper river

Kipchaks—nomadic people living originally on the steppes of modern Kazakstan in southern Siberia. In the 11th and 12th centuries, they took over the eastern European steppes, where they came to be known as the Polovtsy.

Kokand (Khokand)—Medieval and modern city in the Fergana valley, modern Uzbekistan)

Kosika—village on the lower Volga

Krim (Solhat)—Medieval city in the Crimea. Now called Staryi (Old) Krym

Krivaia Luka—dry river bed and locality on the lower Volga River

Krym—see Krim

Kubok—vessel found in a burial that undoubtedly was used for a cultic purpose

Kufic—stylized script primarily used during the early Islamic caliphates and frequently found as an architectural decoration

Kulikova—battlefield where the Russians first defeated the Mongols in 1380

Kumiss — (kumys) a drink made from fermented mare's milk

Lvov—city in western Ukraine

Majar—city of the Golden Horde period in the northern Caucasus

majolica—ceramic technique in which the body of the vessel is coated with white engobe before being decorated with painted images, glazed, and fired.

Mamay—emir and de facto ruler of the Golden Horde in 1380

Mariognoli, Giovanni—papal envoy to China in 1338

Massagetae—nomadic tribes of eastern Iranian origin, who inhabited the western part of Central Asia in 1st millenium B.C.E.

Mengli Girei—khan of Crimea 1469—1515

Mengü Timur—khan of the Golden Horde 1267–1280

Merv (Mary)—ancient and Medieval city in Central Asia, near the modern city of Bayram Ali in Turkmenistan

mihrab—niche in the wall of a mosque oriented toward Mecca

Mokhsha—fortress of the Golden Horde period in Mordvinia

Moncastro—see *Aq-Kermen*

Möngke—grandson of Genghiz Khan and supreme ruler of the Mongol Empire 1251–1260

Mongols—13th century nomadic people of Central Asia who were one faction of the Mongol empire. After they settled widely in the West they were called Tatars

Moscovia—name often applied to Russia in western Medieval sources

Moshchevaia Balka—Medieval burial ground in Alania located in the Caucasus

New Sarai (Sarai al-Jadid)—second capital of the Golden Horde, constructed in the 1330s

niello—metallurgical technique in which the surface of a silver object is decorated by inlaying a black alloy.

Nizhnii Arkhyz—site in the Caucasus, the remains of the Medieval capital of Alania

Novgorod—self-governed city in Russia

Ogödäi—third son of Genghiz Khan and Great Khan of the Mongols from 1229–1241

Orda—headquarters of a nomadic leader

Orda of Sarai—name of the mobile headquarters of the Golden Horde khans on Fra Mauro's map

Ordos—area in Inner Mongolia

Ossetians—people of eastern Iranian group descendants of the Alans who live in the Caucasus

Otrar—Early Medieval city and oasis in the Syr-Darya basin that was an inportant trade center on the Silk Route; now in the territory of western Kazakstan.

Özbeg—khan of the Golden Horde 1313-1341

p'ai-tzü—"tablet of power" issued by Mongol khans to officials

Pegalotti, Francesco Balducci—Florentine writer of the 14th century

Piano Carpini, Johannes de—ambassador from Pope Innocentius IV to Güyük, Great Khan of the Mongols

Polovtsy—people of Turkic origin who spoke a language of the Kipchak group. They were the principal inhabitants of the eastern European steppe from the 11th to the 13th centuries.

Prester John—imaginary leader of Central Asian Christians.

pul—copper coin of the Golden Horde and Old Russia

qadi—judge in the Islamic East

qatun—Mongol queen

Qur'an (Koran)—sacred book of Islam

Rubruck, William of (Wilhelm)—ambassador from Louis IX to the Great Khan Mongka of Mongolia

Sa'adi—famous Persian poet

Saka—(also Sakae) tribes of eastern Iranian origin who inhabited large parts of the eastern Eurasian steppe belt from the 7th to the 3rd centuries B.C.E.

Salamat-Girei—khan of the Crimea 1608-1610

Samarkand—ancient and Medieval area in modern Uzbekistan; modern city in Uzbekistan

Sarai al-Jadid (New Sarai)—second capital of the Golden Horde

Saraichik—Golden Horde fortress on the road from Sarai to Khwarizm.

Sarai—first capital of the Golden Horde, also known as Old Sarai

Sarmatians—Indo-Iranian speaking nomadic people, principal inhabitants of the southern Ural steppes, and along the middle and lower Volga and middle and lower Don regions from the 4th century B.C.E. to the 3rd century C.E.

Sawran—Medieval city on the middle Syr-Darya

Scythians—Indo-Iranian speaking nomads, the principal inhabitants of the eastern European steppe from the seventh to the fourth century B.C.E.

Selitrennoe gorodishche—remains of the first capital of the Golden Horde at Old Sarai

Semirechiye—the region along southern Kazakhstan, extending into eastern Uzekistan, watered by "seven rivers" the source of its Turkish name.

Shahr al-Jadid—a city of the Golden Horde period in Moldava

Shams al-Din Muhammad—merchant from Shiraz who traveled to the Volga region in 1438

sharif—religious and administrative authority in the Islamic East

Shash—Medieval name of the Tashkent oasis

Signakhi—Medieval city on the middle Syr-Darya

Sizabul—Greek form of the name of the Turkic khagan Dizabul

Situla—a type of drinking vessel, probably associated with ceremonies

Sogdiana (Sogd)—ancient country in Central Asia locate in the Zaravshan River valleys and along the Kashka-Darya rivers; today in modern Uzbekistan and Tajikistan

Sogdians—people of eastern Iranian origin, principal inhabitants of Sogdiana

spinel—type of semiprecious stone naturally occurring in many colors

Staryi Krym—modern city in the Crimea

Stronello, Pietro—Venetian merchant who travelled to Hajji-tarkhan in 1391-1392

Sudak (Sugdea, Soldaya)—Medieval port and modern city in the Crimea

Sukhumi—Medieval port and modern city on the Caucasian coast of the Black sea

Suzdal—Medieval and modern city in Russia

Synop—trade city south of the Black Sea

Syr-Darya—river in Central Asia flowing into the Aral Sea

Taman—Medieval port on the Taman Peninsula (Black Sea)

Tamerlane (Timur)—emir and the founder of the Timurid Empire in Central Asia and Iran

Tana—city of the Golden Horde era located at the mouth of the Don River Known as Tanais (the Greek name for the Don River) by the Greeks, in Medieval times Tana was called Azaq. Today it is Azov.

Tanguts—people of Inner Asia

Tashkent—Medieval city in Central Asia; the modern capital of Uzbekistan.

Tatars—name often applied to the Mongols by Medieval Western sources; today the people from the Tartarstan Autonomous Region west of the Ural Mountains.

Timur-Qutlugh—khan of the Golden Horde 1397-1399

Tolstaia Mogila—a royal Scythian tomb in modern Ukraine

Toqta—khan of the Golden Horde 1291–1313

Toqtamish—khan of the Golden Horde 1380–1400

Trebizond—port on the northern coast of Asia Minor

Tsarev (Tsarevskoe gorodishche)—ruins of the second capital of the Golden Horde at New Sarai, near the modern city of Tsarev

Turfan—city and oasis in the Tarim basin in Xinjiang Autonomous Region, Western China

Turks—nomadic tribes living in southern Siberia., who in the 2nd half of the first millennium C.E., migrated westward and settled widely in the Central Asian steppes, modern Kazakstan, and eastern Europe.

Ukek—city of the Golden Horde period on the Volga River

ulus—territorial and tribal subdivision of a nomadic Mongol state bestowed on a khan

Urgench—the Medieval capital of Khwarizm

Uvek—village near Saratov in the middle Volga River region where remains of the Golden Horde city of Ukek are located

Variags—name of the Normans in Old Russia

Vodiansk (Vodianskoe gorodishche)—remains of the Golden Horde city of Beljamen, near the modern city of Dubovka north of Volgograd

Volga Bolgaria—country of the Volga Bolgars; modern territory of Chuvashia

Volgograd—modern city on the Volga, formerly Tsaritsyn

Volodimir—duke of Chernigov

Wire drawing—a metallurgical technique in which metal is pulled through a series of apertures in a stone bar; each aperature being smaller than the previous

yam—posting station on the state roads of the Mongol period

Yarkand—city and oasis in the Tarim Basin, Xinjiang Autonomous Region, Western China

yarliq—written order or charter issued by a khan

Ye-lu Tch'ou-ts'ai—Kitan minister of Genghiz Khan

Yenotaevka—a village on the lower Volga

yurt—round portable dwelling used by Kazak and other Turkic speaking nomads (also see *ger*)

Zemarchus—Byzantine envoy to the Turkic Khagan Dizabul

The Selected Bibliography

Artamonov, M. I.
1962. *Istoriia khazar [The History of the Khazars].* Leningrad.

Ballod, F.
1926. *Alt-Sarai und Neu-Sarai, die Hauptstädte der Goldenen Horde.* Riga.

Ballod, F.
1994. *"Tresors des tombes de l'aristocratie sarmate au Nord de la Caspienne."* In *Les Scythes. Guerriers nomades au contact des brilliantes civilisations grecque, pers et chinoise. Le dossiers d'archéologie.*

Egorov, V. L.
1985. *Istoricheskaia geografiia Zolotoi Ordy v XIII-XIV vv. [Historical Geography of the Golden Horde from the thirteenth to the fourteenth century].* Moscow.

Fedorov-Davydov, G. A.
1996. *Kochevniki Vostochnoi Evropy pod vlast'iu zolotoordynskikh khanov [The Nomads of Eastern Europe Under the Rule of the Khans of the Golden Horde].* Moscow.

Fedorov-Davydov, G. A.
1984. *Zolotoordynskie goroda Povolzh'ia [The Golden Horde Cities in the Middle Volga Region].* Moscow.

Fedorov-Davydov, G. A.
1984. *Städte der Goldenen Horde an der unteren Wolga.* Munich.

Fedorov-Davydov, G. A.
1976. *Iskusstvo kochevnikov i Zolotoi Ordy [The Art of Nomads and the Golden Horde].* Moscow.

Fedorov-Davydov, G. A.
1972. *Die Goldene Horde und ihre Vorgänger.* Leipzig.

Fedorov-Davydov, G. A. 1984. *The Culture of the Golden Horde Cities.* Oxford.

Grekov, B. D. and A. Iu. Iakubovskiy
1950. *Zolotaia Orda i eë padenie [The Golden Horde and its Fall].* Moscow-Leningrad.

Heyd, W.
1986. *Histoire de commerce du Levant au moyen age III.* Leipzi.

Howorth, H.
1986-1986. *History of the Mongols. I-III.* London.

Kramarovskiy, M. G.
1985. *"Serebro Levanta i khuddozhestvennyi metal Severnogo Prichernomor'ia XIII-XV vv. (po materialam Kryma i Kavkaza) [Silver of the Levant and Artistic Metalwork of the Northern Black Sea area from the thirteenth to the fifteenth century (based on materials from the Crimea and the Caucasus)]." Khudozhestvennye pamiatniki i problemy kul'tury Vostoka.* Leningrad.

Poluboiarinova, M. D.
1978. *Russkie liudi v Zolotoi Orde [Russian People in the Golden Horde].* Moscow.

Polo, Marco
n.d. *The Travels.* Translated from the text of L. Benedetto by A. Ricci. With an introduction and index by S. D. Ross. London.

Risch, F.
1930. *Johan de Plano Carpini.* Leipzig.

Risch, F.
1934. *Reise zu den Mongolen 1253-1255.* Leipzig.

Spuler, B.
1965. *Die Goldene Horde. Die Mongolen in Russland 1223-1502.* Wiesbaden.

The Additional Bibliographic Sources

Bosworth, Clifford Edmund
1966. *The New Islamic Dynasties. A Chronological and Genealogical Manual.* Edinburgh: Edinburgh.

Alston, Thomas T.
1987. *Mongol Imperialism.* Berkeley and Los Angeles: University of California Press.

Ch'ang-ch'un
1976. *The Travels of an Alchemist. The Journey of the Taoist Ch'ang-ch'un from China to the Hindukush at the Summons of Chinghiz Khan, Recorded by His Disciple Li Chih-Ch'ang.* Translated with an introduction by Arthur Waley. Westport: Connecticut: Greenwood Publishers: 132.

Frye, Richard N.
1988. *The Heritage of Central Asia: From Antiquity to the Turkish Expansion.* Princeton: Markus Wiener Publishers.

Giovanni di Pian di Carpine
1989. *Storia dei Mongoli a cura di P. Daffin, C. Leonardi, M. C. Lungarotti, E. Menest, L. Petech. Spoleto:* Centro Italiano di Studi sull' Alto Medioevo: 283, lines 178–187.

Grousset, Rene
1970 (1996). *The Empire of the Steppes: A History of Central Asia.* Tr. Naomi Walford. New York: Barnes and Noble.

Ibn Battuta
1962. *The travels of ibn Battuta A.D. 1325–1354.* Translated with revisions and notes from the Arabic text, ed. C. Defremery and B. R. Sanguinetti, H. A. R. Gibb. Vol. II. Cambridge: Published for the Hakluyt Society at the University Press: 515-16, 494-96.

Kipling, Rudyard
1977. *Rudyard Kipling's Verse. Definite Edition. London and Toronto:* Hodder and Stoughton: 234.

Menander the Guardsman
1985. *The History of Menander the Guardsman.* Introductory Essay, Text, Tr. and Historiographical Notes by R. C. Blockley. Liverpool: Francis Cairns: 47.

Munkuev, N. Ts.
"A New Mongolian P'ai-tzü from Simferopol." *Acta Orientalia Academie Scientiarum Hungaricae,* Tomus XXXI (2): 185-215.

Pegolotti, Francesco Balducci
1936. *La Pratica della Mercatura, edited by Allan Evans.* Cambridge, MA: The Medieval Academy of America.

Rubruck, William of
1967. *The Journey of William of Rubruck to the Eastern Parts of the World, 1253–1255,* as narrated by himself, with two accounts of the earlier journey of John of Pian de Carpine. Translated from the Latin, and edited, with an introductory notice, by William Woodville Rockhill. Nendeln/ Liechtenstein: Kraus Reprint Ltd.: 27–29.

The Secret History of the Mongols
1982. Frances Woodman Cleaves (Tr. and Ed.). Cambridge, Mass. and London: Published for the Harvard-Yenching Institue: Harvard Unviversity Press, Vol. 1.

Swietoslawski, Witold
1999. *Arms and Armour of the Nomads of the Great Steppe in the Times of the Mongol Expansion (12th– 14th Centuries).* Lodz: Oficyna Naukowa.

Index

A

A-shih-na family 19
  legendary ancestor 19
Afars 18
Ahura Mazda 12
akhi
  brotherhood of craftsmen 82
Akhtuba River 3
Al-Kalkashandi
  geographer 42
al-Omari
  Arabic writer 72
al-Sara 71
al-Umari
  Arab geographer 42
Alania 21, 23, 24
Alanian cemetery
  Moshchevaia Balka 23
Alans
  Ossetians
    Sarmatians 23
Alexander the Great 12
Alexandria 6
Almalik 46, 48
Amazonia
  mythical 36
Ampasalak
  silversmith 13
Animal Style 15, 19. *See also* art
Aq-Kermen 40
Arab 23
Arab caliphate 24
Arab Muslims
  war with Crusaders 28
Arabia 25
Aral Sea 21
architecture
  from Crimea 91
Argonauts 11
armament 82
armed cavalryman 14

Armenian king Artawazd 13
art
  Siberian 15
Astrakhan 3, 10. *See also* Hajji-tarkhan
Avars 18
Azaq 36, 41, 42, 55, 82
Azov 85
Azov, Sea of
  harbors 42

B

Bactria 16
  Bactrian workmanship 16
Balducci Pegalotti 48
  on trade with the Golden Horde 39
Batu (Khan) 27, 28, 66, 70
  and Sarai 35
  appearance of 88
  description of 88
  founder of Golden Horde 38
Beljamen 36 *See also* Vodiansk
Berke (Khan) 90
Black Sea 6, 10, 11, 16, 18, 21
  harbors 42
  Silk Road 24
  steppes 24
Black Sea ports
  trade routes 23
Bolgar 24, 36. *See also* Volga Bulgaria
Bolgars 38
Bosporus 10
brick workshops 78
Buddhist
  manuscript 24
Buddhist monk Hsüan-tsang 21
Byzantine 18, 25, 40, 44
  architecture 24
  embassy 22
  envoys 22
  Zemarchus, envoy 22
Byzantium 18, 19, 20, 33

envoys 22
shipping 21

C

Caffa 40
caliph of Baghdad 29
caliphates
   Arab 23
caravansaries 45
Catalon Atlas of 1375 34
Caucasus 16, 21, 24, 33, 38, 43
   conquered by Mongols 25
   northern 23, 36
cauldron
   Roman cauldron 13
Central Asia 6, 10, 15, 16, 18, 19, 23, 24,
   26, 31, 32, 37, 38, 45, 46, 47, 49,
   52, 64, 71, 79, 96
   alternate trade route 46
   captured by Mongols 25
   Crown of Monomakhos
      origin of 50
   Central Asian workshops 16
   Hun's military campaigns 18
   Mongol migration from 26
   Nestorian Christian in 27
   Piano Carpini in 28
   Sarmatian military activity 10, 13
   Shahan Shan's armies 22
   silk 5
   Silk Road in 25, 32
   source of information 33
   trade routes through 6, 21
   ulus of Chagatai 27
Central Europe 10
Ch'ang-ch'uen. *See* K'iou Ch'ang-ch'uen
   and Genghis Khan 32
   return route to China 33
Chernigov
   looted 70
Chernyi Yar 3
China 5, 6, 18, 19, 21, 23, 24, 32, 71
   captured by Mongols 25
   pilgrims 21
   technical progress, lead in 99
Chinese coins 20
Chingizid

empire 27
family 27
Christians 72
Cleopatra 6
coins 46, 53, 55. *See also* mints
   Baghdad 47
   Chinese 48
   dirhams 56
   Edigei
      monetary reform 56
   Egyptian 47
   Feodosiya, from 53
   Girei Dynasty 53
   Indian 47
   Jöchid 55
   Khwarizm 57
   mints 55
   silver horde from Tatarstan 53
   Sultans of Delhi 58
   Toqtamish
      monetary reform 56
   type of images on 57
   Urgench 47
Colchis 11
Constantinople 40
   envoys 22
   trade 22
Crimea 10, 32, 33, 38, 71
   conquered by Mongols 25
Crusaders
   war with Arab Muslims 28

D

Danube 9
dictionary
   multilingual 47
dinars 53. *See also* coins
dirhams 56
Dizabul 22. *See also* Turkic kaganate
Dmitri Ivanovich
   Russian commander 96
Dnieper River 24
dugout
   symbol of slave status 65
Duke Jaroslav of Suzdal 29
Duke Michael of Chernigov 29

E

eastern Europe 24
Edigei
   monetary reform 56
Egypt 43, 44
Ektag
   Golden Mountain 22
enslaved craftsmen 63
Europe 6
evil spirits 22

F

female burial: *See* women
Ferdinand von Richthofen 5
Fergana 18
fire 22
Fra Mauro's of 1459. 34

H

Hajji-tarkhan 35, 43, 98. *See also* Astrakhan
hedgehog
   in Siberian and Central Asian art 15
Hellenistic art 12
Heraklea 9
Herodotus 15
Hindukush 6
horse 10, 14, 16, 18, 22, 23, 28, 29, 33,
   39, 45, 46, 47, 61, 67, 69, 78, 85, 86
   as food 87
   bridles 10, 16
housing
   aristocratic 67
   nomadic 69
   at Old Sarai 74
Hsiung-nu 18
Hsüan-tsang 21
Hulägu (Khan) 27
Huns 10, 18
   Hunnic invasion 17
   military campaigns
       with Byzantium 18
       Iran 18

I

Ibn al-Athir 39
Ibn Battuta 71, 82, 86, 89

India 6
Indonesia 6
Iran 5, 6, 13, 16, 19, 20, 21, 23, 25, 32,
   33, 43
   captured by Mongols 25
   coins to Golden Horde 46
   Khan Hulägu 27
   Sassanid Dynasty 22
iron mines 22
iron-smelting 49
Itil 24

J

Jand 36
Janibeg (Khan) 36, 42, 89, 95
Japan 6, 32
Jety-su 18. *See* Semirechiye
jewelry
   Italian influence 45
Jöchi 27, 36, 57
Jöchids 36, 55, 57
Jurchen 50

K

Kama region 24, 25, 36
Karakorum 28
karkhanah 79
Kashghar 21
kashi, ceramic body 49
Kazakhstan 6, 14
Keldibeg (Khan) 58
khagan 19 *See also* great khans
   Turkic 22
khaganates 19, 20
   eastern and western 20
   Turkic 21
Khazar workmanship 25
Khorezmshahs
   state of 26
Khotan 21
Khwarizm 21, 28, 32, 36, 43, 45, 46, 48, 55
Kiev 28, 41
Kiliya 40
kiln 78
K'iou Ch'ang-ch'uen. *See* Cha'ang-ch'uen
Kipchaks 31, 42
   troops and slaves 42

Kokand 21
Korea 6
Kosika 10, 14, 15, 17
  cylinder seals from 12
  burial site 10, 15
Krim 40, 42, 82, 93
Krim (Solhat) 36
Krivaia Luka 9
  burial 9
Kuban River 21
Kublai (Khan) 27
Kuldja 21
kurgan 10

L

Lake Baikal 9
Lake Balkhash 21
Languedoc 41
Lop-Nur 21

M

madrasa 92
Majar 36, 85, 89
maps
  and fantasies 35
Marco Polo 31
  father Niccolo and uncle Maffeo
    alternate route to China 32
  route to China 32
Marduk 12
Mediterranean Sea 6, 42
merchants
  multinationality 40
Mesopotamia 6, 12
  conquered by Mongols 25
Middle Ages 11
Migration Period 19
military outposts 48
mint. *See also* coins
  minting coins
    right of the khans 57
  at New Sarai 55
missionaries
  from western Europe 93
Mokhsha 36
Moldova 36

Moldovan
  archeological sites 41
  trade route 40
Moncastro 41
money *See also* coins
  in the form of silver 24
Mongka (Khan) 27, 66
Mongols 17
  art
    Chinese motifs in 49
  as Tartars 37
  dwellings 29
  empire 27
Mongol dynasty in China 27
Mongol Iran
  Tabriz 46
Mongolia 6, 9, 10, 20, 26, 32
  Mongols conqueror 25
Mordvinia 36
Moscovia 36
Moshchevaia Balka 24
  Alan Cemetery 24
mosques 90
  at Selitrennoe 91

N

Naples 41
Near East 12
  trade 10
Nestorian Christians 27
New Sarai 43, 96
  destruction of 96
  excavations 65
Nizhnii Arkhyz 24
  arts and crafts center 24
  Byzantine artifacts 24
  temples 24
northern steppe route 21
Novgorod 27

O

Ogödäi 27
orda
  as mobile headquarters 37
Orda of Sarai 36
Ordos 10

plaques 10
Ossetians 23. *See also* Sarmatians: Alans
Otrar 28, 32, 46, 48
Özbeg (Khan) 69, 95

P

p'ai-tzü—a 58. *See also* Symbol of authority
Palestine 6
Paquette
    French slave in Mongol court 66
Peking 27
Persian 18
Persian Gulf 6
Peter the Great 14. *See also* Siberian Collection
Piano Carpini 28, 63, 82
    and Batu 28
    and Güyük 29
    appointed Arshbishop 29
    Embassy of 28
Pietro Stronello
    Venetian merchant 43
Pizzigani in 1367 34
Poland 41
Polovtsy 31, 33, 38. *See also* Kipchaks
    burial mounds 48
    nomads 27
Prester John 27, 28. *See also* Nestorian Christians
Pskov 27

R

Red Sea 6
religion
    Ahura Mazda 12
rich household 84
rise of cartography 34
rituals 15
Roman 16, 18
    craftsmanship 12
Rubruck, William of 30, 40, 66
    and Batu (Khan) 30
    and Möngke (Khan) 30
    description of effigies 31
Rudyard Kipling 5
Russia 24, 27, 33 38
    conquered by Mongols 25

princes 66
regalia 50

S

Saka epoch 17
Samarkand 24, 32
Sarai 35, 42, 43, 48, 55, 60, 72, 86, 95
Sarai al-Jadid 60
Saraichik 36, 43, 45, 46, 48
Saratov 36
Sarmatian 9, 10–12, 15, 17, 23
    aristocracy 16
    art produced in Bactria 16
    burial 38
    chieftain or priest 11, 13, 15
    epoch 17
    legends 10
    military campaigns 11
    rise in power 10
    steppe 10
    warrior 10
    weapons 15
Sawran 36
Scandinavia 24
Scythians 9, 10, 15, 19
    chieftain 11
    nobility 11
    epoch 17
    tongue 22
Sea of Azov 6, 21
Selitrennoe 3, 44, 47, 48, 51, 73, 74, 76, 78, 84, 85, 88, 90
Semirechye 18 *See also* Jety-su
Shahr al-Jadid 36
Shams ad-Din Muhammad
    merchant 46
Shash 21
Siberia 14
    petroglyphs 19
    art 15
    nomads 15
Siberian Collection 14 *See also* Peter the Great
Signakhi 36
silk 5, 6, 20, 22, 23
    icons, painted 24
    in burials 24

in Byzantine workshops 24
in Moshchevaia Balka 24
painting in China 24
silk production 5
Sogdian 24
Silk Road 5, 6, 17–20, 28, 32, 38
blocked 23
during Turkic period 20
enters new age 25
near Black Sea 24
second route 6
southern branch 6
third route 6
Silk Route. *See* Silk Road
silver coins
Russia 24
Scandinavia 24
Volga Bulgaria 24
Simferopol 58
horde 58
treasure 59, 92
Sinope 40
Sizabul 23
Slave-craftsmen 64
slavery 42, 63
described by Piano Carpini 64
in manufacturing 79
Sogdia (Sogdiana) 22, 24
St. Mark's Republic 42
Stanitsa Belorechenskaia
burials 44
Staryi Krim 36, 92
Sudak 39, 40
Sultan Salamat Girei 55
Sultans of Delhi 47
coins
trade. *See* coins
Sycophantic envoys 6
Syr-Darya 18, 21, 28, 36
Syria 6, 41
Syrian-Palestinian workmanship 24

T

Tabriz 46
Tamerlane 36, 49, 95, 96, 98. *See also* Timur
Tana
imports to 41
Italian colony 41

sea port on North Black Sea 41
trade with Trebizond 42
Tang Dynasty 21
Tangut 52
Taoist monk
K'iou Ch'ang-ch'uen. *See* Ch'ang-ch'uen
Tashkent 21
Tatars
as Mongols 29
Golden Horde known as 37
Tatarstan 53
Temujin. *See* Genghis Khan
Tereshchenko, A. V. 60, 69
Timur 49, 95. *See* Tamerlane
Timurid
pottery imitating porcelain 49
Tolstaia Mogila 11
Toqtai (Khan) 55
Toqtamish (Khan) 54, 95, 96
monetary reform of 56
Toulouse 41
trade
Adriatic Sea 44
Aq-Kermen 40
Belgorod Dnestrovski 40
Black Sea 43
change in routes 98
China 17, 49
contacts with the West 44
Dniestr River 40
down the Volga 43
Egypt 42, 44, 86
European 44
Far East 14
from China 48
Greece 9, 11, 12, 17
Hindukush 47
Iran 17, 25
Kazakh steppes 21
Kazakhstan 14
Mongolia 17, 21
Near East 17
Nepal 47
Otrar 46
Padua 48
Roman 12
routes 16
Shiraz 46

Siberia 14, 21
Sultans of Delhi 47
Thessaloniki 44
through Crimean ports 40
through Tana 41
Transcaucasia 17
Tsarev 50
Turkey 40
Volga region 21
with Italian cities 41
trade galleys
on Black and Azov Seas 39
trade routes 16, 17, 21, 46
during Great Migration Period 18
to China 48
on the Volga 23
trans-Uralic region 25
Transcaucasia
military expeditions 46
trade 10
Trebizond 40, 42
Tsarev 3, 36, 44, 47, 60, 61, 62, 69, 76, 78, 82, 85, 88, 96. *See also* Sarai
Tunhuang 21
Turfan 21
Turkic
burials 20
khaganates 22, 23, 38
nobility 20
spread of power 19
writing system 20
Turks 19, 22

U

Ukek 36, 55, 88
ulus of Chagatai 27
umbrella
symbol of power 90
Urals 10, 15, 16, 18, 21
Urgench 28, 36, 43, 48
Urumchi 21
Ust-Urt Plateau 21, 45, 46

V

Venice 41, 44, 48

Vodiansk 36, 66, 78, 85, 90, 96.
See also Beljamen
destruction of 96
Volga River 3, 9, 10, 16, 18, 19, 21, 24, 28, 32, 36, 38, 43, 72, 73, 95
known as Edel 35
region as crossroads 17
Volga Bulgaria 24, 36
conquered by Mongols 25
Volga Regional Archaeological Expedition 10, 73

W

weaponry 81
William of Rubruck *See* Rubruck, William of
wolf
A-shih-na family 19
women 66
burial 9, 48, 88
hats 89
jewelry 59
khan's daughter 86
manner of dressing 88
mausoleum at Ukek 88
mirrors
in burials 89
riding horses 29
toiletry items and jewely 89
workmanship
Bactria 30
Byzantine 18
Central Asian 18
Chinese 18
Khazar 25
Syrian-Palestinian 24
workshops
Mongol 64

Y

Yarkand 21
yarliq
imperial edict 66
Yenotaevka 3

Z

Zemarchus 22